The Silent Sell-Out

The Silent Sell-Out

Government Betrayal of Blacks
To The Craft Unions

by Arthur Fletcher

Assistant Secretary of Labor in the First Nixon Administration

THE THIRD PRESS
Joseph Okpaku Publishing Company, Inc.
444 Central Park West
New York, N. Y. 10025

Copyright © 1974 by Arthur Fletcher

Library of Congress Catalog Card Number: 73-83161
SBN 89388-100-7

First Printing: November, 1973

Designed by Bennie Arrington

1800686

Acknowledgments

I want to acknowledge the contribution of Alfred W. Blumrosen, Professor of Law, Rutgers University, who is a noted professor of law whose specialty is Labor and Civil Rights Law. He served as Chief of Conciliation, United States Equal Employment Opportunity Commission, 1965-67 and as a consultant to the Employment Standards Administration at the United States Department of Labor from 1967-72.

It was he who as my consultant encouraged me to keep notes of my daily experiences in the hope that I might want to publish a book once I had served my tenure.

I also want to extend my thanks to Mr. Horrice Menasco, former City Manager of Pasco, Washington, who resigned his city management position and came to Washington D.C. to serve as my Deputy Assistant Secretary and Chief Administrative Officer for the Employment Standards Administration. In addition I wish to thank Mr. John L. Wilks, formerly of San Francisco, California, who closed his own successsful public relation firm to join my staff as Deputy Assistant Secretary and Director of the Office of Contract Compliance.

I also want to mention Mr. Nelson Crowther, a very able administrative lawyer, who served as my Special Assistant for Administration, and Mrs. Vera Lincolin, who served as my Office Manager during my brief, fast-moving stay at the United States Department of Labor.

5

This book is dedicated to my trusting friend and wife Bernyce who has spent many lonely hours and seen very little of me since I took up the cause of equal employment opportunity and the elimination of economic discrimination.

Preface

My purpose in writing this book is to lay before the American people the elements of the struggle for civil rights in employment, to give the history of past failures to realize our own potential and to indicate the "last clear chance" which now lies before us. Perhaps a prefatory word about my own position in the struggle is in order. As a black American I have seen patterns of restriction and discrimination at various points in my life. After I reached the age of 40, circumstances placed me in a position where I could not only see where opportunities for great and real progress in equality lay, but also gave me the opportunity on a small scale, to put these concepts into practice. These opportunities led me to the position of Assistant Secretary of Labor for Employment Standards, with responsibility for the government's equal opportunity program concerning employment by federal contractors. It has been difficult to remain a black government official for a number of reasons, not the least of which has been the inability of the administrative units of government, for which I was responsible, to react quickly enough in dealing with employment discrimination. What is needed now is a sense of the decisive importance of these programs, and the "muscle" inside government to carry them out. I must state that this sense of urgency and this sense of need for decisive action do not now exist, although we are closer to having them than at any time in the history of government efforts in this field. Thus, I believe that a national commitment to enforce equal opportunity can be translated quickly and efficiently into action in spite of the first major efforts at enforcing these civil rights laws.

This may be our last chance to make America into the kind of society envisioned by its principles. Failure now will lead to rejection and repression which will infect all of our institutions. Economic growth and progress will become impossible without the redistribution of income and increasing sense of fairness which will flow from application of the principles of equal opportunity.

I know that the President, the White House, the two Secretaries under whom I served, and many others in the government share the basic views which I have outlined above. But there is an indefinible gap between theory and practice in government, and as of this writing, this gap has not been closed by the present Administration.

Contents

CHAPTERS

Introduction	11
1. Employment is the Key Issue in Civil Rights	17
2. Twenty Years of Failure—1944-1964	25
3. Congress Finally Acts: The Passage of the Civil Rights Act of 1964	41
4. The Johnson Executive Order	47
5. The Newport News Case	49
6. Silent Sell-out: The Failures of 1967-1968	55
7. The Construction Industry, 1969-1971	63
8. Tooling Up the Rest of The OFCC Program	77
9. How to Get the Job Done	83
Appendix A	87
Appendix B	95
Appendix C	101
Appendix D	115

Introduction

This book was completed in the early part of 1972, shortly after I resigned as Assistant Secretary of Labor for Employment Standards, where I had enforced the requirement that government contractors provide equal opportunity. Much of the remainder of the book is devoted to a discussion of the problems of enforcement of this principle, which has been little honored thus far in American history. Here I wish to make another point—a point about the pervasiveness of the race question in America, and how it permeates all aspects of American life. It is not, as some have suggested, solely a special interest issue, posed for the benefit of the minority interest groups, although, of course, it includes that aspect.

Rather, I submit, it is the central domestic question in America, and one of the hallmarks of our reluctance to recognize this fact, is the tendency to put it aside in favor of other issues, or other ways of looking at issues. Yet, the evidence of the 1972 election supports my thesis; for the approach we took in 1969-1971 profoundly influenced the outcome of that election, and reshaped and realigned older political allegiances. This shifting of forces took shape around the "Philadelphia Plan" with its concept that equality of opportunity required minimum numbers of minority participation in government-subsidized work.

This one positive contribution made by the White House to equal employment opportunity during the first four years of the Nixon Administration did more than anything else to bring about a change in the position of two major forces in American politics which traditionally had supported the Democratic Party: organized labor and the organized Jewish community. Both of these groups concluded that their interests were no longer served by such close ties with the Democratic Party, and moved away from the exclusive support for that party. This move assisted the President in winning his overwhelming election victory in 1972. Since then, both groups have reaped some major benefits from their change of position; the Jewish groups in terms of American foreign policy, and the Organized labor movement in terms of revitalized control over the Department of Labor, symbolized by the appointment of a labor man, Peter Brennan, as Secretary of Labor.

Central to this state of affairs was the evolution of the Philadelphia Plan, details of which are described later. The plan came as a series of shocks to organized labor. The first shock was that the plan could emerge within the Labor Department itself. The Labor Department has traditionally been the comfortable home of one part of organized labor; the older craft unions associated with the American Federation of Labor, including, importantly, the construction trade unions. The Bureau of Apprenticeship and Training had been a buffer between the trade unions and pressures to increase minority hiring in the early 1960's. The thought that the department would seriously press for increased minority hiring was, under the circumstances, somewhat unrealistic.

Yet the plan did emerge from the Labor Department. Once it was out, labor lost control over events, and found itself subject for the first time to potentially effective administrative control insisting on increasing minority employment opportunities. This lesson was not lost on the labor movement. A more sympathetic Labor Department would never have set the plan in motion in the first place. Since the rank and file "hard hats" were opposed to this program, the labor movement set out to mend its fences sufficiently with the administration to assure that the Department would not, in the future, take such a pro-civil rights stand that labor's interests would be ignored. This was accomplished by a form of neutrality during the 1972 elections, which gave President Nixon his sweeping victory.

Once the "Philadelphia Plan" had cleared the Labor Department, the labor movement first tried to block it in the Office of the Comptroller General. This move was defeated when the Attorney General issued an opinion upholding the plan. The same message, of the need to see that the administration paid more attention to the labor movement's position, was conveyed in this action.

Labor then tried to defeat the plan by asking Congress to adopt a rider to an appropriation bill which would have outlawed the plan. Again the White House put its support behind the plan, at the same time reinforcing the message to organized labor. But, perhaps more importantly, the labor movement lost control of the principal lobbying machinery on the hill: the leadership conference. This was a loose-knit federation of minority interest groups, mainly organized labor and organized Jewish groups which had, over the years, been the lobbying spearhead for civil rights advances. Labor had played a major role in the group but it was immobilized on the Philadelphia Plan question. It did not wish to offend organized labor, for labor had been a major supporter in many past civil rights battles. Yet it could not support the effort of the labor movement to suppress the Philadelphia Plan. It was immobilized. The result was that the Congress itself was immobilized, and the attempted limitation on the plan was defeated.

Once the plan was issued, events were beyond the control of labor. The courts sustained the plan. Yet it had to be implemented by administration, and labor set out to influence administration. In this, they were joined by portions of the organized Jewish community, which felt threatened by the concept of "quotas" for minority employment. This threat had complex roots, including the remembrance of restrictive quotas, and the fear that minority hiring quotas might harm members of the Jewish community in seeking certain kinds of employment.

The result was that the "quota question" became an issue in the 1972 election, with the President taking a position which tended to restrict the concept as it had been articulated in the Philadelphia Plan. On this question, the McGovern Democratic forces were either "pro quota" or without position during most of the campaign. The clearest message was that of the Republican Administration, which, ironically, won voters by promising to restrict the operation of the only major civil rights initiative it had taken during the first Nixon Administration.

While both Labor and the Jewish groups sought to influence the future administration if the Republicans should win, the minority groups did not. The result was that Nixon was reelected with major debts to Labor and the Jewish community, and virtually none to the black and brown community.

I have said many times that this approach on the part of the "civil rights community" is a mistake, and I fear that the next years of this administration may further document my assertion. This is true because while Labor and the Jewish groups have sought some limited accomodation with the administration, they have not left the Democratic Party. If the Democrats resume power in the future, they will still have important claims on any new administration. The "civil rights community" with its exclusive emphasis on the Democratic Party, has lost the benefit of participation in the Republican Administration, without gaining any corresponding increase in influence in a future Democratic Administration.

In terms of providing for increased minority participation in the economic affairs of the nation, and of achieving equality of employment opportunity, this approach by the civil rights community does not make sense. The struggle for civil rights in America requires hard, sustained and intelligent effort. With that effort, we can succeed, for the basic conditions for success do exist.

But without that effort we can fail, for in the tough hurly-burly of every day political life, crucial decisions affecting the destiny of all of us, are hammered out by intelligent purposeful men and women.

We are entitled to the opportunity to participate in this process —and this by virtue of the electoral and political processes. But we have no assurance of success beyond the competence of our own forces; influences, and intelligence.

Thus, the conclusion of this chapter is that the position of the Administration on the race question during the period covered by this book, had a profound influence on the outcome of the election of 1972, which, in turn, will shape and influence the future of America on issues and concerns that range far beyond the race question, and touch on all Americans.

John Donne's poetic comment that, "no man is an island," has long had symbolic meaning in the struggle for human rights. I submit that it now has practical operational meaning for all Americans. The rest of this book represents my effort to explain that meaning, in terms of the problems and prospects for equal employment opportunity.

CHAPTER ONE

Employment is the Key Issue In Civil Rights

Employment is the key to the solution of the Civil Rights Problem. Employment brings income and individual dignity. It gives a sense of participation in the economy of the nation, and of hope for personal advancement. Income earned through work makes it possible for individuals to make choice. Individual freedom is meaningless without the economic ability to make such choices.

Blacks, particularly, but also other racial and ethnic minorities, have always been viewed in America as workers doing the lowliest of jobs, under the most degrading of conditions. At the founding of the nation there were two kinds of poor workers: indentured servants, who were white, served for seven years and then were freed; and black slaves who served from birth (or from the time of capture) until death. With the end of slavery, the role of black workers as the performers of low and menial tasks persisted. With exceptions here and there, they continued to be the last reservoir of labor, kept in poverty but available for use on "dirty jobs" which whites did not want to do, of they were called upon in times of crisis when, as in World War II, the nation required more manpower.

As a result of the mass migration of blacks from the South into the large cities of the North in connection with both World

Wars and the Korean conflict, the pattern of maintaining blacks in menial work spread from the South. In the North, it took different cultural forms: that of near total exclusion from certain plants and offices, rather than that of mass participation in low skilled jobs. But the schooling and training available to blacks in the North did not equip them to seek and obtain the better jobs. Meanwhile, the southern pattern of restricting blacks to menial and low paying jobs persisted. The most striking remnant of the era of slavery in our century has been the subordinate position of the black man in the job market. This has meant the denial of dignity, income, and sense of participation in the affairs of the nation to generations of black Americans. The injustice of this situation has spawned many efforts in the last quarter century to eliminate the subordinate job market condition of minorities, and to establish a meaningful equality of economic opportunity.

From the beginning of World War II, the rising organizations of blacks and demands of liberal organizations have impressed on government and on society, the importance of equal job opportunities. In 1941, to avoid a march on Washington, led by A. Phillip Randolph, President Roosevelt agreed to establish a committee to deal with the problem. The Supreme Court, in 1944, held that racial discrimination was illegal under the nation's labor laws. The northern states, beginning in 1945, passed fair employment practice laws. The federal government continued and revised its controls on job practices of federal contractors. The Congress in 1964 added employment as a civil right to be enforced under the first major substantive civil rights legislation in a century. These laws and orders have not secured equality of employment opportunity.

With the failure of these laws has come the increasing loss of hope for the future among blacks and other minorities—particularly, among the youth, who live in a permanent state of depression. This hope for the future is an integral part of our attachment to our society and its institutions, and the loss of it generates, particularly among the young, an alienation form the values of our society. This alienation means one thing to black American youth, and quite a different thing to white society. To the black youth it is stultifying. It destroys hope, makes serious work seem futile, and leads toward a rejection of the fundamental values of the American society.

This seeming rejection of work by black youths in a culture of which they cannot be a part, is the origin of one of the worst white racist stereotype views of Blacks as lazy, unwilling, surly people "to be kept in their place."

Thus, the denial of employment opportunity not only influences the black community, but shapes the entire white society, and crystallizes sharp differences in attitude toward both the race problem and the values of society itself.

Whatever may be the merits of "black capitalism" or other forms of minority improvement programs, the fact remains that we are increasingly in an employment society. More of us than ever work for others. This pattern has been sharply accelerated in the last 40 years, and can be expected to continue. Thus, denial of access to good employment opportunities is far more serious a restriction today than it was when the frontiers of individual economic endeavor were open.

For example, in many northern areas, minority employment in suburban plans is low, or nonexistent. If that employment were increased, the pressures for minority suburban housing would increase. The opportunity to educate children in suburban educational institutions rather than in the rat holes of the cities, would open up to men and women who had the economic resources to afford suburban life. In the South, if promotional opportunities were opened to the black men and women in the steel industry, their ability to provide for the education of their children would be enhaced, so that the next generation would move up in the economic world, rather than remain at the same point on the wheel of life where fortune had cast their parents.

It is often said that there is a vicious circle of discrimination in housing, education and employment, and that nothing can be done unless all three are attacked equally at once. Some say nothing can be done in one area until the other two are corrected, others say nothing can be done at all short of revolution.

I say that the problem can be solved; that the Gordian knot can be cut; and the way to cut it is to open up employment opportunities. There are a number of reasons why this is essential:

1. American society views a man through his work. Work

means dignity, opportunity for promotion and money. Not to work means failure, dropping out, alienation, rejection, anti-social thoughts and actions.

2. Work opportunities tie men and women to the society, just as ownership of land by farmers in the frontier period bound them together as a nation.

3. Work opportunities can be provided within the existing institutions of the American economic, social and political system. All of us are skeptical and suspicious of "make work" programs, or "special employment projects" which do not play a part in the basic economic system of the nation. These are usually failures. They produce "training programs" which do not lead to jobs. Worse than that, they are viewed by many blacks as attempts by the white man to buy the black man off cheaply. Thus, they are not taken seriously as work opportunities. The failure of most of such programs is testimony to the fact that a solution to the civil rights problem is the opening up of the existing institutions to minorities. Devising special "preserves" or "reserves" for blacks appears only as a sop to a noisy political minority, not as a recognition of the right and dignity of each as an American citizen. Only our massive economic system can supply the employment opportunities necessary to establish the individual equality which the civil rights concept requires.

4. The expansion of the economy predicted for the 1970s makes the expansion of minority work opportunities a real possibility with minimum dislocation of the existing work force. It is the least divisive way to eliminate the remnants of slavery.

5. It is the only productive way to eliminate our civil rights problems. Men and women at work contribute to the national economy. They do not detract from it. Their skills and abilities become a national asset, not a liability to be subsidized at the expense of the rest of society.

6. Work opportunities are viewed by all sectors in the struggle for minority rights as crucial. The work of the NAACP during the last quarter century has been directed in important measure at increasing work opportunities, particularly in the construction industry. At the other end of the spectrum of the struggle are the Black Panthers. Often forgotten in the recent spectacular series of confrontations between armed Panthers and armed po-

lice, is point two of the ten point program of the Panther party, which reads:

We want full employment for our people: We believe that the federal government is responsible and obligated to give every man employment or a guaranteed income. We believe that if the White American businessmen will not give full employment, then the means of production should be taken from the businessmen and placed in the community so that people of the community can organize and employ all of its people and give a high standard of living.

7. Confidence in government, and in our social institutions, will return quickly if there are results. We have passed the stage where anything less than visible improvement of the position of the minorities will be considered to be of any value to those who criticize our institutions. Results can feed hope, can encourage initiative, study and diligence.

8. With increased employment opportunity, members of minority groups can take advantage of existing opportunities for education and improved housing. They can become a vocal political force for the improvement of society in general, dealing with those other problems which face us all as Americans—the improvement of the quality of life. Unfortunately this participation at the moment is subordinated to the struggle for civil rights.

The time necessary to substantially accomplish these objectives is no more than two years. The legal tools in the form of statutes, executive orders and court decisions supporting such programs as my Philadelphia Plan, are now in existence. The administrative procedures for implementing these laws and plans have now been drawn up. It only remains to put them into effect. Discrimination, not the lack of education, is responsible for most of the inferior positions of blacks in the labor force. By ending the pattern of discrimination quickly, we will solve a good part of the problem. To end the subordination of blacks and other minorities what I propose is not a long-range plan (which would tend to perpetuate it) but a short-range one to end it. Otherwise, I foresee an increasing escalation of discontent and disaffection on the one hand, and an increasing withdrawal and alienation of many, both white and black, on the other. Our form of government depends on consent and participation. Over the last five years, more and more citizens, of all races, have considered withdrawing their consent to be governed, and have withdrawn their participation in the ordinary affairs of our society. We may be at a critical turning point in the history of the nation, retesting the question framed by Lincoln at Gettysburg: whether a nation founded on principles of equality can long endure.

The youth of our nation are prepared to reject the society which we have built, in part because of its indecent treatment of minorities. The question is whether we have the will—and the time— to leave them a society which in fact operates on principles of decency.

Let us now turn to the dismal history of our generation's efforts to deal with discrimination in employment: a history in which no institution, no government, no party, and few individuals, emerge as entitled to plaudits for a job well done; a history of repeated opportunities to end discrimination which were lost. The reader will see that political partisanship is misplaced in consideration of this history. For example, the Democrats led the fight for the Civil Rights Act of 1964, but it was Republican Senator Dirksen who made the statute a workable tool, over the objection of the Democrats. Though the laws and orders of the 1960s were on the books, the Democratic Administration failed to implement them. If these laws and orders had been enforced, they would have brought about orderly change.

The Republican Administration, having now cured the defects in the governmental structure inherited from the Democrats, has the potential to carry out the policies so clearly written in laws and executive orders. Whether this potential will be realized in time to save the nation is the unanswered question. We shall know soon enough.

The next chapter will describe the failures of both the federal and state government to deal with employment discrimination in those crucial decades after World Warr II. The situation which existed in 1964-65 was a direct result of these unsuccessful efforts during the previous periods to cope with the vestiges of slavery in the subordinate position of minorities in the labor force. The following three chapters will deal with the creation of the modern federal anti-discrimination program through laws and executive orders in 1964 and 1965, and with the primary example that, properly enforced, these laws and orders would work effectively to end discrimination. Chapter VI describes through the use of official reports, the actions of the Johnson Administration and its failure to implement these laws and eliminate employment discrimination.

We will conclude on an uncertain note: The Nixon administration took office in January 1969, and began to realize the enormity of the legacy of ineffectiveness left by the Democratic Administration in this area. Internal steps to correct these defects have been taken, and they will be described. But the final question, whether the new revitalized machinery will be in fact used to put and end to the scourge of employment discrimination, remains to be answered.

CHAPTER TWO

Twenty Years of Failure—1944-1964

For twenty years after World War II, the Federal and State governments tried unsuccessfully to cope with empoyment discrimination. Their failures set the stage for the civil rights movement of the 1960s. Here, we will briefly chronicle the ineffective efforts during that period. Our intention is to be objective. There is little point now in attacking the personal motives of those who organized the struggle for equal employment opportunity. The best that can be said for that army of well intentioned, largely white persons who worked during this period, was that they vastly underestimated the difficulty, the tenacity, of discrimination in America. They were led into mistake after mistake through reliance on inappropriate analogies to other problems and other solutions. At the end, they recognized that new tools, new ideas, and often new men, were needed. But the effect of each such mistake was to further compound the difficult position of black and other minorities and aggravate the distance between the preachments of law and the actual conditions of life of minorities. The failure of these employment and equal opportunity programs made it clearer and clearer to larger and larger numbers of blacks and whites that "law and order" meant, not equal enforcement of all laws, but vigorous enforcement of those laws which suppressed black people, and the non-enforcement of those laws designed for their benefit. No wonder that the entire socio-legal structure was finally called into question in the weary days toward the end of the 1960s.

The story which this chapter must tell has three aspects, because there were three separate efforts by different organs of government during these twenty years to fight employment discrimination. They all failed, but for different reasons. The first effort was made by the Supreme Court of the United States, the second by the northern "liberal" State governments, and the third by the President of the United States.

A. The Supreme Court

In 1944, ten years before the desegregation decision concerning schools in *Brown* v. *Board of Education,* the Supreme Court outlawed racial discrimination in employment where a union represented employees. This was in the famous case of *Steele* v. *Louisville and Nashville Railroad,* which reached the Supreme Court in 1944. In that case, the Brotherhood of Locomotive Engineers and Firemen had insisted on changing the terms of the agreement between the union and the railroad so that black firemen could never get to be engineers, and would ultimately be eliminated from their jobs. The black workers sued, and the Supreme Court declared in ringing tones that racial discrimination by a union which secured from a Federal law its rights to represent all workers was illegal. Furthermore, management could not rely on union action based on such hostile discrimination against black workers. Thus was born the "duty of fair representation" under which unions are supposed to treat fairly all employees whom they represent and may not discriminate, or participate in discrimination under collective bargaining agreements.

But nobody paid attention to this ruling. If unions and employers had acted in 1945 to carry out the mandate of the Supreme Court in the *Steele* case, none of the later statutes or executive orders of the 1960s would have been necessary. We would not be in the crisis of civil rights. Employment opportunities throughout the land would have been much more fairly distributed. All of the problems of promotion, transfer and layoff of black workers under collective bargaining agreements which have involved so much effort and so many cases since 1965 would have been solved and eliminated.

26

The unions continued their illegal conduct, and continue some of it today. It is important to remember today (when some companies and some unions try to defend these arrangements on the grounds that "it takes time" to end discrimination) that they have had twenty-five years—more than half the working life of the average worker—to stop violating the law.

The doctrine in the Steele case was not recognized and therefore not obeyed by companies and unions during this twenty-five year period. It had little effect on general practices of discrimination in collective bargaining, which affects twenty to twenty-five million workers.

Its main importance today, however, is not just to show that the law did not work but rather, that the practice which are illegal today and have been illegal for twenty-five years, must be stopped *now,* and that the systems of seniority which discriminate must be changed *now,* and also that the companies and unions responsible for subordinating black, Mexican American, women and other minorities, must pay damages for past wrongs and in addition correct the systems for the future. A quarter century of illegality must not be condoned.

But we may ask why the unions and companies ignored the *Steele* doctrine and continued to subordinate minority workers. Perhaps we may never know the full answer to this question, but we do know parts of it.

First, the pattern of racial prejudice and discrimination, particuarly in the South, after the end of World War II was deep and vicious. Although black soldiers had fought well during the war, and black workers had labored well to produce the weapons of war, once it was over, the nation wished to return to "business as usual," and to resume the pattern of life which it had inherited from the era of legal slavery. None of our institutions in the 1940s was as sensitive as they are now to the race problem. The military was not integrated until after the war, and we still have problems of segregation with respect to housing and other activities for servicemen. In short, the nation, especially the South, was ready to go on just as before. It did not want to hear the call of the Supreme Court to change these long established ways.

Secondly, to whites, the long established patterns seemed to be reasonable. They did not believe that they were engaging in illegal activity, therefore there was nothing to change. Their first response to the decision in the Steele case was to limit it to workers in the railroads and airlines, because the case arose under the Railway Labor Act. The Supreme Court had to make it clear, in 1955, that the decision applied to all workers represented by unions under the National Labor Relations Act. The Southerners thereupon sought to narrow the scope of the doctrine. They finally conceded that they might have to "take the first step" toward equality, by allowing seasoned and experienced black workers to apply for "white jobs" as if they were new employees. To do this, black workers had to give up their seniority and pension rights, their protection against layoff and discharge, and often had to accept lower wages. This was of course, a phony offer as far as most black workers were concerned. They were raising families, and could not risk taking a less secure, lower-paying job, which, to a white man, promised a better future. They knew too well that white employers and unions, bent on perpetuating the subordinate status of blacks, would find ways to get rid of the uppity Nigger, who had the audacity to take a white man's position.

Yet the companies and the unions managed to persuade the highly influential Court of Appeals for the Fifth Circuit in the Witfield case that this kind of "first step" toward equality was "enough" under the doctrine of *Steele v. Louisville and Nashville Railroad Company*. The Court was so impressed that it wrote in its opinion in 1959 that "angels could do no more." In fairness to Judge Wisdom, who wrote that opinion, I should state here that ten years later, in 1970, he wrote an opinion for the same court holding that stronger and more effective remedies were required under the Civil Rights Act of 1964.

Thus, the "bite" was taken out of the *Steele* doctrine by a decade of legal maneuvering, that left black workers in little better condition than they had been before the Supreme Court spoke.

A third reason for the failure to enforce the "duty of fair representation" lies in the lack of litigation. Supreme Court decisions are not self-enforcing. Each injured partly is entitled to sue to secure his rights, and he may sue on behalf of a group or class that is injured. But until such a suit is brought, and won, the law is not enforced unless the companies and unions voluntarily move to comply with it.

We have already seen that such voluntary compliance was not in the cards. But why was there not more litigation?

In the early 1950's all of the litigation strength that the Civil Rights movement could muster went toward fighting for the school desegregation decision which was to come in 1954 and 1955. There were few lawyers concerned with civil rights at the time, and those that were had their hands full with the school cases.

The decision to seek to strike down the segregated schools rather than concentrate on opening up employment is one which, today, we might wish to reexamine with the benefit of hindsight.

The decision was the product of a group of brilliant NAACP lawyers, centered around Howard Law School, which developed and implemented a plan to destroy the "separate but equal" doctrine. Under the banner of "separate but equal", the Supreme Court of the United States had permitted the South to perpetuate many of the vestiges of slavery. The legal attack on this doctrine was conceived during the depression of the 1930's when a quarter of the labor force was unemployed. Under those circumstances, the selection of education rather than employment opportunity as the target for legal attack seemed sensible. Furthermore, there was, at that time, no legal concept which prohibited outright racial discrimination if they wanted to. There was simply no right to any kind of equality in private employment, separate or otherwise. The Fourteenth Amendment with its promise of equal protection applied only to "state action", but not to "private action." Therefore, the attack on the "separate but equal" doctrine had to deal with governmental activities, such as public education, voting, political parties and the like. The public sector thus became the target for the legal activities which culminated in the case of *Brown* v. *Board of Education,* which led to the decision that separate school facilities are inherently unequal, and led ultimately to the destruction of that insidious doctrine.

After the school segregation decision had been won in the Supreme Court, there came the era of "all deliberate speed" of desegregation, and lawyers were busy across the land trying to parry the thrusts of the segregationists who sought to continue their past practices.

In the early 1960's a few cases were filled under the *Steele* case doctrine, but by then, the Court of Appeals of the Fifth Circuit, which covers the deep South, had decided the Whitfield Steel case, and victories would not be likely to produce major pay-offs in any event.

In short, the *Steele* doctrine did not achieve much. It showed the good intentions of the Supreme Court in 1944, but the Whitfield Steel case of 1959 was the "all deliberate speed" formula for employment discrimination. The private law suit under the *Steele* doctrine, during the period we are considering, simply never emerged as an effective weapon against discrimination.

There remains still one question. Even if the NAACP lawyers were busy with school cases, why didn't black and other minority workers have their own private attorneys go to court to enforce their rights? The answer to this question requires a brief examination of the attitudes of black Americans toward the legal system on the one hand, and of the legal services available to them on the other.

The black man has long seen the law as the instrument for his suppression. Slavery was not only permitted by law, but was maintained by constant legal pressures with respect to fugitive slaves and the like. After the Federal occupation of the South ended in 1877, the southern states used the law to continue to keep blacks in conditions akin to servitude. To black Americans, the law meant segregated facilities and eating places, poor working conditions while in general, they were supposed to be nice to white folks. They would not look to the law for help, because they did not believe that it would aid them in the struggle against discrimination. This attitude persists down to the present day. Only a small percentage of those blacks who are subject to illegal discrimination will complain to legal authority. Thus the unwillingness of the black community to use the law is one of the current problems facing administrators of civil rights programs.

If the black worker had gone to a private attorney during this period, what kind of help would he be likely to get? Here, another form of racial discrimination produced a substantially blind alley. There were few blacks in the legal profession. It was largely a white man's monopoly throughout the country. This disastrous tradition is only now beginning to be corrected. When one has listed the handful of brilliant, distinguished and successful black attorneys during that era, the dismal fact remains that most black attorneys were the product of poor segregated law schools, had received a poor legal education and served poor clients of minor matters. Few of them would have been able, by training or experience, to cope with the difficult litigation against the experienced lawyers of management and labor. This litigation was conducted before unsympathetic white judges who had to be persuaded to apply the *Steele* doctrine. This meant that black workers had to seek the aid of white lawyers, and in a few cases this aid was. forthcoming. But the most experienced white lawyers in the field were the representatives of labor or management. They would normally not take a case against the group which they represented. Thus, a private law suit in that period would have gotten the complainant nowhere.

Furthermore, the cost of litigation was too prohibitive for a poor black worker to want to carry a case of doubtful validity through the courts. The fact that he was held to a low-paying job prevented him from developing sufficient funds to bring litigation which, if successful, would have permitted him to earn more money. The wheel of discrimination turned against the black worker. So much for the attempt by the Supreme Court to eliminate employment discrimination in collective bargaining.

B. The State Fair Employment Practice Commissions, 1945-1964

In 1945, New York and then New Jersey, adopted State Fair Employment Practice Laws. These laws were copied in some twenty states by the end of the twenty-year period we are discussing. None of the states which adopted these laws was in the South. They were the liberal states in terms of civil rights issues. The laws represented an attempt to prevent the emergence of the southern pattern of discrimination, and to eliminate the patterns of discrimination which had already grown up in the North, Northwest and West. This pattern had emerged as a result of the influx of black workers during the war, and as a result of ethnic and religious discrimination against Jews, Irish, Italians and others.

If these laws had been realistically meaningfully enforced, they would have ended the typical northern style of employment discrimination which is simply the continuation, in subtle form, of the southern pattern of assigning blacks to the dirtiest, hardest, lowest paying jobs and also, totally excluding them from many facilities and operations. For example, many of the suburban production facilities erected during the period after the war were staffed almost exclusively with white workers. During this period, white-collar employment opportunities outnumbered for blue-collar employment. Yet, blacks were excluded from most white-collar jobs. The State Fair Employment Practice Commissions did little or nothing to halt this trend.

Why the failure? The answer here is different from that in the preceding section. Most of the state laws established administrative agencies, usually called commissions, which were charged with investigating, and hearing cases of job discrimination. They had to power to issue "cease and desist orders" to prohibit discrimination, and they had or acquired the power to act on their own initiative without waiting for a complaint. They were modeled after the National Labor Relations Board, which protected the rights of workers to organize.

With all these legal tools there seemed to be no reason why, unlike the *Steele* doctrine, the agencies should not have succeeded.

The black worker did not need his own lawyer. He did not bear the costs of proceeding. The FEPC would process his case for him. The philosophy of these laws was that the agency would be a kind of father figure, helping the poor blacks who were unable to help themselves.

The failure of these agencies may be laid to the philosophy of paternalism that pitted the agency unsuccessfully against the economic interests of employers and unions. We Americans are rightly suspicious of paternalism. The individualism which infects us and our institutions is an essential aspect of our culture. Self help has been the method of advancement of all peoples who have come to America. Benevolent paternalism usually ends up with the beneficiaries in worse shape than before the "aid" was given.

The concept that honest, sincere and dedicated state administrators could somehow "lift" the black people to new levels of income and dignity under these statutes, in retrospect, looks almost humorous. When the efforts of the administrators clashed with those of employers and unions, the administrators failed. Employers and unions clearly understand that their interests lay in maintaining the status quo. They had the political, economic and legal muscle to make their views prevail in State government. But there was rarely any such conflict between the Commissions and employers or unions. The men and women appointed to these commissions were selected to be "sensitive" to the position of employers and unions. Thus the administrators took the "bite" out of their own laws in a variety of ways:

1. They narrowly interpreted the statutes, so that they could not act until the civil rights groups had persuaded the legislature to pass amendments to the laws. This enabled the administrators to put off effective enforcement programs until the legislature had acted again, which is known as "passing the buck".

2. They adopted a policy of "education" rather than enforcement" and viewed their task as evangelical, rather than law enforcement. They would lecture the offending employer or union on the proper form of conduct, and consider that they had done something worthwhile. They acted on an incredible philosophy that since one could not change morals by law, it was necessary for the law to permit discriminatory conduct.

3. As a result of this approach, they accepted "soft settlements" rather than adopt effective remedies to change systems of discrimination and help those who complained of discrimination. These settlements often consisted of nothing more than a promise to do good in the future, without admitting that the respondent had ever done anything wrong.

4. Because of the political difficulties involved, they failed to act against important employers who practised discrimination but against whom there had been no complaints. And this in spite of the fact that they had the power to do so.

5. They feared to take employers or unions to public hearings, even though they had the power to do so, and preferred to settle for little or nothing rather than try to enforce the law. As a result, only a handful of hearings had been held in these twenty states at the time of the passage of the Civil Rights Act of 1964.

6. They did not have a working definition of discrimination, which is perhaps the most incredible failure of all. The agencies were so timid that they did not create sharp issues against which the courts could act to define employment discrimination. When the 1964 Civil Rights Act and the 1965 Executive Order where adopted, we began for the first time to define what discrimination really meant. The FEP agencies had swept the most crucial issue of all under the rug.

Thus, the issue of discrimination was never faced by the fair employment practice commissions, and was not clearly faced at all until the period of the modern statutes and executive orders.

But how did it happen that a perfectly good law was perverted so as to permit the continuation of discrimination?

First, the staffing of these commissions was done under political guidance of the governor's offices of the various states. Commissions tended to have businessmen and labor union officials and lawyers as appointees, on the grounds that they were most familiar with the problem. This was, of course, only partly true. They were familiar with the problem from the perspective of the white man running the institution which was discriminating, not from the perspective of the black victim of discrimination. Where blacks or other minorities were appointed, they were usually either ministers (who believed in education and moral suasion rather than law enforcement) or persons who were deeply involved in the political activity of the party doing the appointing. When appointed, they saw themselves as being directly responsible to the governor, not to the black community, and the governor, of course, was politically more responsive to labor and management, than to the black community. Thus, the lack of continuing political pressure by the black and liberal community made a farce of the legislation which had been passed by the liberals in the post World War II era.

This experience should have taught two important lessons to the civil rights community. First, a "powerful agency" with "cease and desist" powers, can be rendered impotent by the personnel who administer it and their policies. Second, if legislation is to be implemented, the civil rights community must maintain continuous day by day surveillance over programs and maintain pressure on the staff, To ensure that there is serious effort to carry out the law. The recent liberal drive for "cease and desist" powers for the EEOC seems to ignore this lesson altogether.

Finally, to make sure that the agencies did not get very far, the state legislatures restricted their budgets, thus denying them the effective manpower necessary to do an adequate job, and providing the administrator with a built-in excuse for his failure. This is known also as "passing the buck."

C. The Federal Government Contractor Program from World War II to 1964

The first Federal Fair Employment Practice Commission was created in 1941 by President Roosevelt to "head off" a march on Washington by angry black workers headed by Phillip Randolph. It did little, and was allowed to lapse in 1974. In 1951, President Truman established a new commission, which President Eisenhower continued as the Committee on Government Contractors during his Administration. The same failure to adopt an enforcement approach dogged these agencies during the period of the 40s and 50s as has been described with respect to the state agencies. Despite a few successes, the federal program made no serious inroad into racial discrimination during that time.

By the end of the Eisenhower Administration, it was clear to those in Washington, including the Vice President, Richard Nixon (who was in charge of the program) that stronger measures were needed, that the voluntary approach had not worked. When President Kennedy was elected, he began a "new era." He toughened up the Executive Order, and made real enforcement possible. The threat of the government terminating business with a contractor who discriminated was used to dissuade contractors from practicing discrimination.

Since almost all of the nation's large and influential employers are government contractors, an effective tough-minded enforcement program by the Federal Government, could have destroyed the pattern of discrimination if not in the first hundred days, at least, during the first two years of the Kennedy Administration.

The new and tough Executive Order not only prohibited racial discrimination by Government contractors, but also required them to take affirmative action to assure equal employment opportunity. The program was kept, under the Kennedy order, under the direct supervision of the Vice President. It operated through an institution known as the President's Committee on Equal Employment Opportunity. The legal tools were sharp and clear in the Executive Order. In addition, the office was placed under the influential leadership of Vice President Johnson. On paper, it looked like the most effective tool yet devised to end job discrimination. However, it was gutted as soon as it was created.

The seemingly powerful tools of the Kennedy Executive Order were blunted by the creation of an organization of large employers, known as "Plans for Progress." When civil rights legislation is rendered impotent, the action usually takes place behind closed doors, but in this case, it was out in the open. "Plans for Progress" was openly presented as an alternative to the enforcement approach suggested in the Executive Order.

There was public discussion of the matter. At issue was our old friend "education" rather than "enforcement." This time it was dressed in slightly new clothes, called "voluntarism." The idea was that the big corporations would undertake a voluntary program of affirmative action to improve the lot of black workers (more paternalism again) and thereby would avoid the enforcement procedures which otherwise seemed available under the Executive Order.

By the end of 1961, the issue had been resolved. Plans for Progress was established as a "complement" to the enforcement program, in the face of the fact that the existance of PFP undercut any notion of significant law enforcement. "Plans for Progress" was administratively financed by the Government.

This meant that an organization of employers which, in effect, helped to hold off Government enforcement efforts in the anti-discrimination field, had a staff in Washington paid for by the Government while their businesses publicly advertized their "voluntary programs" to end discrimination.

Note that the Government did not finance any organization of black workers to achieve the same result. Once again, the fate of black workers was left to the paternalistic benevolence of the

Government. Only, this time, it was left to the judgement of the very corporations which had engaged in discrimination and had made possible the situation which called for correction.

The nature of a voluntary plan is that it must be acceptable to the planner. It must "fit in" with his overall strategy. Most employers' overall strategies were concerned with profitable production. The development and existence of the pattern of discrimination was consistent, in their view, with profitable production. Thus, any voluntary plan could be counted upon to continue the essential pattern which the employer had established, making superficial "token changes" to avoid any more serious inroad on company discretion.

The only way to alter this result would have been to establish that the employer's overall strategy for profitability would be defeated if he continued to discriminate. This would have required an enforcement effort to make him recognize that he would lose money and profiitable Government contracts if he persisted in discrimination.

Only under those circumstances would "voluntarism" or "enlightened self-interest" lead the employer to stop discriminating. But "Plans for Progress," by eliminating the enforcement approach virtually guaranteed that employers would do little to alter the pattern of discrimination in the land.

Despite some exceptional example of good citizenship, "Plans for Progress" (PF) was a dismal failure. From 1961 to 1968, it proved to be a plan for prejudice, rather than a plan for progress. Its main achievement consisted in the holding of big meetings with employers, some of which took on party-like atmospheres, with participants congratulating each other on what a great job they were doing. Finally, their "cover" was blown by the Equal Employment Opportunity Commission (EEOC) in 1968. In hearings on white-collar discrimination in New York City, the EEOC disclosed that PFP companies had a worse record of employment of minorities in the city than those companies which had never belonged to any voluntary organization to improve minority employment. In 1969, after the Republican Administration took office, PFP was quietly folded into the National Alliance of Businessmen (NAB), whose major program (JOBS) was designed to, and did secure work for the hard core unemployed. It therefore had some credibility as a workable instrument. PFP just quietly dissolved.

It is clear from the example of PFP that "Voluntary Programs" will not end discrimination. Trying to "educate" the discriminator to realize that what he is doing is wrong will not end discrimination. The lesson is as clear as the "all deliberate speed" formula in the school cases.

Perhaps there were some who actually believed that the "voluntary approach" could work. If so they were naive as to the toughness of the problem or confused over the meaning of the word "voluntary" which in American life, does not always imply "uncoerced." As to the toughness of the problem, nothing need be said other than that we are still fighting the shadows cast by the institution of slavery which was abolished 105 years ago. It is important to note here that discrimination cannot be abolished through coercion alone and that some amount of goodwill (which is voluntary) is also necessary.

"Plans for Progress" persisted however, and the 1960's saw the greatest explosion of civil rights legislation in America in 100 years. The Civil Rights Acts of 1964, 1965, and 1968 established the legal rights of blacks, other minorities and women to be free from invidious discrimination. But the administration of these laws was inadequate to carry them out. The details of this story however, cannot be gone into now. Suffice it to say that the situation, in the early 1960's, with Plans for Progress undermining the enforcement of the Kennedy Executive Order, did not change quickly even when Congress began to adopt civil rights statutes. The story of political influence on the administration of legislative programs is an infinitely complex one. Part of this story will be told in later chapters.

The relevant point here is that most people in the middle and upper echelons of government are very "sensitive" to what they believe to be the views and policies of a wide range of people— their superiors, the head of their agency, the president, and the appropriations committee which rules their destiny. As long as they believe that some or all of these people have a "go slow" attitude toward changes in civil rights programs they will be very cautious. In fact, they might be far more cautious than their superiors, and sometimes they will do things which are contrary to what their superiors want. Sometimes they are completely wrong about these attitudes in the first place. But the nature of the bureaucracy makes those who work in it intensely conservative. Thus, a cautious program once put into effect is very hard to change in the direction of a more effective system, without changing the individuals who are responsible.

For example, the old Presidential Committee on Equal Employment Opportunity, which operated from 1961 to 1965 with Plans for Progress, was abolished in 1966 in favor of the Office of Federal Contract Compliance with a "tougher" enforcement approach. But it appears a good number of PCEEO people simply transferred to the new agency, taking with them their cautious non-enforcement oriented attitudes.

Thus, the presence, in influential places in government, of important men who were opposed to the civil rights program imposed a regime of caution on the entire bureaucracy. And this contributed to the caution shown by the Administration without there ever being any direct show of political muscle or influence. To search for an individual "devil" in the form of "some congressman or administrator who was opposed to civil rights as an explanation of the failure of government, is to miss the point. It is the entire range of pressures and influences, real and imaginary, bearing on the conduct of each official of government which led to this caution.

The bureaucrat's sense of caution is further justifiied by a hard look at who succeeds in climbing the bureaucratic ladder within government. Is it the imaginative, aggressive, dedicated man who presses hard, or is it the cautious, careful individual who rarely, if ever, sticks his neck out? History has demonstrated that, for a bureaucrat, caution pays, and courage shown leads to either a dead end, or dismissal in some reorganization. The story of Gerard Clark, which will be told in a later chapter, is evidence for this statement. Experience has taught these bureaucrats that caution is better than courage from the perspective of personal life advancement and survival. Thus, does a cautious program continue.

Another factor which seriously troubled me during the time I served as Assistant Secretary of Labor is the lack of adequate numbers of competent effective men and women to carry out courageous and effective programs. Many of the problems of employment discrimination are difficult and complex from a technical point of view. Production processes, seniority systems, a tangle of legal and informal rules must be understood and evaluated in terms of their consequences for minority opportunity. Labor and management have adequate numbers of highly competent specialists in law, labor relations and the like. Their sheer intelligence and knowledge may frustrate a less competent government person. Frequently, weak programs continue because the Government simply does not know how to do better. It does not have the manpower to out-think, out-negotiate, and out-maneuver labor and management, to achieve equal employment opportunity.

All of these factors contributed to the failure of the Kennedy Executive Order, and the dominance through the period 1961-1965, of Plans for Progress.

CHAPTER THREE

Congress Finally Acts:
The Passage of the Civil Rights Act of 1964

The decade of the 1960s began with violence and ended in turmoil. The early sixties saw racist white southerners in their last ditch "stand in the doorway" against desegregation in schools; it saw freedom riders taking humiliating punishment; saw a black lady refuse to move to the back of the bus and magnificent men like Rev. King reaching to establish, in fact, the equal dignity which the law had long promised the black man. It saw a Jewish and a Black youth buried in the lonely woods by racist murderers in Mississippi and a white woman with an Italian name gunned down on the road from Selma to Montgomery. August, 1963, brought the long delayed march on Washington for civil rights: the same march which Phillip Randolph had wanted to lead in 1941.

President Kennedy had made the passage of civil rights laws including provisions against employment discrimination a part of his program. He died by violence before it was adopted. In the summer after his death, Congress passed the first substantive civil rights law in 100 years. The Act covers public accomodations, voting and other matters as well as employment discrimination.

We are concerned only with Title VII of the Civil Rights Act of 1964, which deals with job discrimination. The Act was passed after a long filibuster and went into effect on July 2, 1964; but most of its provisions were not operative until one year later. The reason for the delay was twofold: to give industry and labor an opportunity to come into "voluntary compliance" and to enable government to "tool up" for the jobs of enforcing the statute. Neither of these objectives was achieved. Industry and labor did not come into "voluntary compliance," and the government did not "tool up" to secure compliance. But this story must await an explanation of some of the crucial elements in the legislative maneuvering behind the passage of the Civil Rights Act of 1964.

The bills which provided the foundation for the law against discrimination in employment were generally modelled after the state "fair employment practice" legislation which had proved such a dismal failure. They prohibited various forms of discrimination on the grounds of race, color, religion and national origin, and provided for an administrative agency which could investigate, conciliate, and, if necessary, hold an administrative hearing and issue specific remedial and preventive orders. The form that these orders usually took was to compel the respondent to "cease and desist" from his illegal conduct. This phrase "cease and desist" became the rallying cry for those who were in favor of these original bills and the administrative procedure they embodied.

As the days of legislative maneuvering and debate dragged on, this question of "cease and desist" powers became one of the central issues in the debates. Finally, in order to secure a compromise which would end a filibuster, and assure the adoption of the civil rights bill, the "cease and desist" powers were dropped. After this bit of legislative surgery, the agency was empowered to investigate, and, if cause existed, try to conciliate. If conciliation failed, the complainant could file suit in federal court, but there was no administrative hearing procedure. The courts could issue broad orders if they found discrimination. Suit in court could also be initiated by the Attorney General.

This "truncated" administrative agency was to be called the Equal Employment Opportunity Commission (EEOC) which had the power to request reports on racial composition of the work force, give technical assistance, and perform other administrative functions.

Civil rights supporters thus gave up "cease and desist" powers, in order to secure the bill which was passed. They have always viewed this as a "defeat" and have continually pressed for amendment to the law to give the comission "cease and desist" powers.

This has been a strange upside down struggle. Congress had opened the court to equal opportunity claims, yet the "liberals" wanted administrative hearings. The plain fact is that administrative hearing procedures had failed to work in the civil rights field for a quarter century. The reasons the "liberal" supporters of "cease and desist" powers wanted to join this tradition are obscure The way it has worked out, the courts have been rendering good decisions under the Civil Rights Act of 1964, and the EEOC is bogged down in its own procedures. If the liberals had "won" the fight for "cease and desist," we would not be as far along as we are in the struggle for equal oportunity. Thus, the opponents of cease and desist, led by Senator Dirkson, performed a great service for the minority community by saving it from its friends. An all powerful administrative agency is a will-o'-the-wisp, a myth, and has possibilities for built-in failure. All the conservatives need do is "capture" the all powerful administrator, and the program is destroyed. This was the lesson of the state agencies, and of Plans for Progress. But the "liberals" oblivious of this, sought to repeat old mistakes. Fortunately, they were saved from this blunder.

The other compromises necessary to end the filibuster and secure the passage of the employment discrimination section of the 1964 Civil Rights Act, were mainly verbal, designed to make sure that prohibitions on discrimination in seniority and testing did not become a basis for general regulation of those subject matters. One compromise which has caused some difficulty is the so called "no quota provision," which, I believe, is designed to (a) make sure that there is an instance of discrimination before remedial action can be ordered under Title VII and (b) to suggest that rigid mechanical solutions to complex and subtle problems must be avoided. Beyond that, the "no quota provision" is not meaningful as will be seen when we come to discuss the Philadelphia Plan and the difficulties it ran into with regard to this.

There was one more important amendment to Title VII, which has lasting repercussions. Some have said that Representative Smith introduced "sex" as a prohibited ground for discrimination in employment, in order to defeat or confuse the bill, and in order to confuse the administration of any law which was adopted. Whatever his motives, sex discrimination was made illegal in Title VII, and the provision has stimulated much concern in the last five years for women's rights, both in employment and elsewhere. The subject of women's rights in employment is sufficiently complex and difficult to deserve separate treatment, both in connection with Title VII and in conecction with the Executive Order which I administered. We will not discuss it further here, except to note that the same problems of stereotypes, of restriction to work in certain jobs and the like, which are basic to race and ethnic discrimination arise in connection with women's employment.

Thus the statute which emerged from the Congress did not adopt the principle of paternalism, which had for so long dominated thinking about how these statutes should be written. For Senator Dirkson's primary point had prevailed in the debates. This was to preserve the individual right of aggrieved black workers to sue in federal court if their claims could not be settled by conciliation. Here was a modern statute which was based on the principle of self-determination by black and other minority workers. They, not some white administrator, would decide if the efforts to end discrimination were sufficient.

The question of costs of private litigation was also with in the statute. The courts may award attorneys fees to prevailing plaintiffs. This is an important, if little known, section. Usually, in America, each party pays his own attorney fees. If I win $10,000 as damages in an automobile accident, my lawyer may well take one-third of this as his fee. But the judge or jury which set the verdict at $10,000 did not include anything for my lawyer.

A provision of Title VII made it possible for a winning black worker to keep all of the damages he was paid. The losing employer or union was made to pay his attorney fees—*on top of* the damages due the worker. This was encouragement to private litigation because it assured a victorious plaintiff's lawyer a fee.

The NAACP and the Legal Defense and Education Fund, Inc. were able, by the passage of Title VII, to develop a litigation program. They expanded their legal offices, and started many suits, knowing that, in the long run, a good portion of the expense of such an organized program would be borne by those guilty of discrimination.

The mood of the black and other minority workers of the nation began to change. They began to complain to the EEOC and then to file law suits under the Act.

The courts, believing that Congress intended to end discrimination under the Civil Rights Act of 1964 began to render vigorous decisions on a number of points favoring minority workers.

Thus, the defects of the individual right to sue, discussed earlier with respect to the doctrine of *Steele* v. *Louisville and Nashville Railroad Company,* simply did not apply to the proceedings under Title VII. Viewed with hindsight, then, the decision to recognize the individual right of black workers to litigate, was a good decision, and promised more benefits to the civil rights movement than paternalistic "cease and desist" pattern of legislation which had failed. Under Title VII, as it was administered, government officials could not determine for the black worker what was good for him. Secret deals between government officials and employers or union representatives were not possible, because the black worker had to sign an agreement before there could be a settlement. The government officials could not dispose of the claims of the black workers through the soft settlements which sounded nice but gave no results. This was a great advance for civil rights over the previous system, and its existence is due to Senator Dirkson's insistence on avoiding "cease and desist powers," and substituting the individual right to sue in the Civil Rights Act of 1964.

It may be argued that all of these developments came after Title VII was passed: that the EEOC could have interpreted Title VII to allow the government and the respondent to settle cases without the agreement of black workers; that the NAACP and the INC Fund might not have developed legal programs. It is true that only in hindsight is Senator Dirkson a truly important positive force in the civil rights program. His reputation was that he was against civil rights enforcement programs. But his decision to accept the final bill was crucial to its passage, and the procedure of the private law suit to its passage, and the procedure of the private law suit provided significant old fashioned individual rights which were long overdue to the black worker.

The effort to secure the passage of the statute had been tremendous. The "Leadership Conference" of labor, the NAACP and other civil rights groups which had fought for the legislation were exhausted by the effort.

The Congress had given the President power to appoint the five commissioners of the EEOC, but they had also given a year's grace before the EEOC had to act. The President himself allowed ten months to elapse before he appointed the commisioners. They took office only a little more than a month before the statute was to go into effect and had very little time to plan, to organize a staff, or to develop a philosophy or a program. The commission has been constantly under the pressure of the backlog of complaints and charges which as a result of lack of advance preparation and adequate staffing, it has not been able to handle properly.

The year 1965, was crucial in the history of civil rights enforcement for the rest of the decade. The commissioners were finally appointed, and the President's Committee on Equal Employment Opportunity was abolished. Its functions were transferred to the Labor Department under Secretary of Labor Wirtz, who had been a staunch supporter of civil rights. A new institution to coordinate all government programs, called The President's Council on Equal Opportunity was created in March, 1965 and Vice President Hubert Humphrey, known for his support of civil rights since he first challenged the southern control of the Democratic Party at the Convention of 1948, was placed in charge. In June, the President gave his famous Howard University speech, in which he showed more understanding, and proposed more supporting action for the black man than had ever been seen before.

In July, Watts erupted.

Then in August, in his Rose Garden speech at the White House Conference on Equal Employment Opportunity, convened under Title VII, President Johnson gave the first major "law and order" speech of our era. He spoke of the preservation of property and peace, not of the achievement of civil rights.

In September, the President's Council was abolished, and some of its coordination functions tranferred to the Justice Department. From that time on, Vice President Humphrey played no major role on the Administration's civil rights policy.

CHAPTER FOUR
The Johnson Executive Order

On the same day that the President's Council was abolished, President Johnson issued his new executive order prohibiting discrimination by government contractors. This was the order which abolished the old President's Committee, established the Office of Federal Contract Compliance, and placed its administrative responsibility in the hands of the Secretary of Labor.

OFCC was to be the small policy making office in Washington which would organize the federal effort to prevent discrimination by government contractors. The primary task of OFCC, however, was not to deal directly with government contractors, but to supervise the activities of the so-called "predominant interest agencies". The idea was that each major contracting agency would be responsible for seeing that government contractors with which it did business kept to the equal employment opportunity guidelines. Where an employer had contracts with more than one agency, the agency with which it did the largest amount of business would have jurisdiction. This system was very awkward but had been developed because, in earlier years, Congress had refused to appropriate funds to support a government contractor program. Therefore each agency had to develop its own program from its own funds if there was to be any federal program. Coordination of this multi-agency program was under the direction of a committee headed by the Vice President from the beginning of the Eisenhower administration until 1965.

During the Eisenhower period, the Committee on Government Contracts had no enforcement power. In 1957, Richard Nixon had suggested that each of the agencies charged with enforcing its program utilize its own enforcement power, but nothing came of the suggestion. During the Kennedy era, the President's Committee, as we have seen, became the victim of the Plans for Progress approach.

In September, 1965, President Johnson dissolved the President's Committee and an executive order transferring direction of the program to the Secretary of Labor.

The Kennedy Order adopted the proposal set forth by Vice President Nixon, on a broad scale. It established powers in the federal government to cancel, terminate contracts, and to debar corporations from bidding on contracts on grounds of employment discrimination. It also required government contractors to take "affirmative action" to ensure that equal employment opportunity existed. The definition of "affirmative action" became important only after the "Plans for Progress" approach was abandoned. Prior to that time, affirmative action largely meant what the corporations involved wanted it to mean.

However, although the OFCC small and remained an organization mainly to coordinate and direct the performance of the contracting agencies its transfer to the Department of Labor gave promise of the dawning of the era of enforcement of civil rights with regard to employment.

This was cause for optimism about the chances of securing, for the first time in our history, the effective enforcement of the civil rights of minority workers in our society. Congress had passed a new statute, creating a new EEOC. It was "talking tough" although it seemed to carry no stick. The federal "big stick" was now in the hands of avowed civil rights supporters in the Department of Labor, who adopted a "tough minded" enforcement oriented approach. The optimism was, however, guarded. The two programs of the EEOC and OFCC had to undergo their first major test. It came in the case involving the Newport News Shipbuilding and Drydock Company of Newport News, Virginia.

CHAPTER FIVE
The Newport News Case

The occasion for the first major test of the effectiveness of the whole structure—EEOC, OFCC and Department of Justice—came early in 1966 in the case of the Newport News Shipyard. The system did, in fact, work in that case. Some three thousand black employees received promotions, and nearly 100 were made or listed to become foreman. An elaborate agreement spelled out the details of what the company was required to do, and an independent expert approved by the government was brought in to do some technical studies which the government was not equipped to do, but would not let the company do by itself. One commentator called this agreement "One Brief Shinning Moment in the Enforcement of Equal Employment Oportunity." It is fair to say that it was "one" and "brief," because it was not repeated during the next two years of the Johnson Administration.

I think it is important for us to see why the Newport News Agreement did work, so that we can better understand why that approach was not used again.

First, it worked because all three agencies did, in fact, cooperate. They put their best men to work on developing the specific written detailed proposals to submit to Newport News. Inter-agency bickering, which became so common later, had not reared its ugly head at the time the agreement was negotiated. That came later, when there were squabbles about who was to get credit for it.

Second, there were enough technically able men in the government service, who knew enough about both industrial relations and racial discrimination, to design a program which would, in fact, improve the position of the black workers.

Third, there were great numbers of black workers who had been held back in promotions by reason of discriminatory patterns, who were readily identified once these patterns were lifted, and were given immediate advancements in their jobs, or were identified for promotion to foreman.

Fourth, the individual right to sue under Title VII had been invoked by the black workers, and the company must have been aware that it could not negotiate a successful "secret arrangement" with the government. The procedure of the EEOC at that time prohibited such secret arrangements. EEOC indicated that there could be no settlement without the approval of the complainant. Therefore, the complainant had to know what the terms of the settlement were.

Fifth, there was a hard-working and dedicated NAACP chapter in Newport News, Virginia, headed by an employee of the Shipyard, Rev. Fauntleroy, who applied day-to-day pressure for equal opportunity, on the shipyard, and then on the government.

Sixth, the OFCC did, in fact, flex its great economic muscle. The Shipyard was told that it would get no further government contractors until the matter was resolved. There has been constant criticism of OFCC for not cancelling the contracts of companies which have been discriminating. However, the technique of preventing them from getting future contracts can be just as effective or even more so. Large corporations operate on a set of assumptions about the continuing nature of their underlying business relations with the government and other major purchasers. This long-term relation may be more important to them than making money on a single contract. Newport News Shipyard actually did 75% of its business with the government. Thus, the threat to cut off future government business with the shipyard was a potent one.

Seventh, in the face of all of the above pressures, the shipyard decided to sit down and negotiate a reasonable agreement, rather than fight to the end. The shipyard's resources were enormous. The yard had access to highly talented legal counsel. They could have fought the government in court and sought an injunction against the Secretary of Labor's decision not to allow them any more contracts until they negotiated a softer settlement and then reneged in carrying out the agreement. They chose to do otherwise.

They fought hard, but they did work out an agreement, and, subject to differences of opinion about what it meant, they kept the bargain they had made.

There was another complicated factor in the picture. The Union was not initially party to the negotiations, but did later acquiesce in the agreement. The tough problems of discrimination in seniority systems which have plagued this field did not exist in any marked form at the shipyard, because there was no uniform seniority system for promotions or layoff. Promotion and lay-off were largely at the discretion of the company. Thus, the level of Union resistance to the actions of the government was lower than it might have been if the Union had had more stringent seniority provisions in the collective bargaining agreement with the company.

The detailed agreement with Newport News, and its administration in 1966-67 set a new high standard for government performance and programs to end discrimination. It looked as if we were on our way, as last, to end the subordinate status of minorities in American life, in an effective and rapid way. True, there were limitations in Newport News. Not all of the problems at the shipyard had been solved, because some had not been fully identified. Those unsolved ones were left to future negotiations. But the basic issues of restrictions on promotions to foreman, (called quarterman in the yard) and on the rate of pay and promotional rate of most minority workers had been dealt with effectively. The government had learned how to end employment discrimination.

If it had then applied the experience of the Newport News case in its dealings with the five hundred largest corporate employers in America, we would have a vastly different nation today in terms of civil rights and individual dignity.

But as the old testament makes painfully clear, fundamental lessons about human rights and human relations are not readily accepted. Newport News was not repeated. The bickering that broke out among government officials, the reluctance of many in government to participate in wide-scale programs against discrimination, the resistance to this concept by management groups, the failure of the President to say "This is the way," and the failure of the civil rights groups themselves to insist on such programs, meant the end of this approach.

The Defense Department refused to participate in such efforts in connection with another large employer. The Department of Labor's OFCC could not function without the assistance of the Defense Department while the EEOC was too weak to single-handedly embark on the task. And so, the question of whether the program would continue or not was resolved in the Department of Defense, which, at the time, was concentrating on the build-up in Viet Nam. What did the Defense Department do?

Firstly, it reorganized the equal opportunity program, took its internal operations away from the office of the Secretary of Defense, and scattered them so that the officials who were responsible for the production of goods which the military needed were also responsible for the equal opportunity program as it affected them. This reorganization meant that procurement of military goods was first, and equal employment opportunity had to be second. Any corporation which could show that equal opportunity programs were hurting its ability to produce for the Defense Department would get a sympathetic hearing, and the equal opportunity program would be subordinated. More specifically, any time a suggestion of stopping government contracts was made, the decision had to be approved by officials who were more interested in the military hardware than in civil rights.

Secondly, the reorganization permitted the Defense Department to dispense with the services of the key man in the previous set-up. This man, Girard Clark, had been an avid exponent of the tough-minded enforcement approach. He had led the way to the contract suspension at Newport News. His approach and his personnel operating out of the office of the Secretary, were, indeed, scaring the industry. After the reorganization, he found himself counting paperclips and looking out of his window. He finally left government in disgust in 1968, calling a press conference to point out how the Johnson Administration had destroyed an effective equal opportunity program.

The EEOC which had played the major role in negotiating the Newport News agreement was also reorganized. Interest in the shipyard waned, and the government paid no attention to the yard until 1969 or 1970. At that time, it was found that the other problems not addressed by the 1966 agreement had matured, and required further action.

Having been in government for some two years, I can better understand some of the elements which went into the bureaucratic shambles which emerged after Newport News, and I can understand some of the reasons why that experience was not followed up. But I cannot justify them. There was credit enough to go round on the Newport case. There was good reason to keep the tough-minded approach of Girard Clark, and there was good reason for the EEOC to continue its role as monitor of the agreement, and to demand that this sort of thing be done more frequently.. Finally, the matter was so important that it should have been taken to the White House, and to the President, if necessary. During my term we went to the White House on several occasions, and we secured the help of the President personally, in one instance (the Philadelphia Plan) where it was critical. At no time did President Johnson ever personally intervene in the equal opportunity programs to make them more effective, or to assist them when they ran into the kind of difficulty which the Philadelphia Plan faced in 1970.

After the Newport News experience, the governmental agencies fell into a period of ineffectiveness and despondency which was not to be dispelled until President Nixon was elected in 1969. The tragedy of these two lost years for the Civil Rights movement, and for the country, is not yet fully clear. But the story of the failures of the federal program during those years has now been fully documented by the United States Civil Rights Commission in its report entitled *The Federal Civil Rights Enforcement Effort (1971)*. It it time to see what happened as the government failed to use the powers, procedures and techniques, which it had forged so effectively in the Newport case.

CHAPTER SIX

The Silent Sell-Out:
The Failures of 1967-1968

The most clearly brutal expose of the failure of government to carry out its function ever written is not by Ralph Nader, but by the U.S. Civil Rights Commission. It is entitled *The Federal Civil Rights Enforcement Effort*. Its review of this period, describing the background of the federal enforcement effort, is a must reading for those concerned with Civil Rights. This review was based largely on an examination of government files, and interviews with hundreds of government employees, past and present.

In this chapter, I can only summarize the dreary story of inept inaction which characterized most of the period of 1967-1968. With each of the three agencies, the story is somewhat different.

A. The Justice Department

You will recall that the Civil Rights Act of 1964 gave the Attorney General the power to sue in federal court to eliminate patterns and practices of employment discrimination. This law was passed on July 2, 1964. At that time, the Civil Rights Division in the Justice Department was given the responsibility to implement it, along with its other responsibilities in the field of school desegregation, voters rights, housing programs, and the protection of the civil rights of individuals against police brutality and other forms of illegal action. The problems of employment discrimination are significantly different from the problems of school desegregation or voter registration. Even lawyers well versed in school desegregation cases might know absolutely nothing about seniority systems or discriminatory recruitment systems. And so, it would have been logical to set up a separate unit in the department, bring in some experienced lawyers who were knowledgeable in industrial relations as well as in civil rights, and organize an enforcement program. This however, did not happen. Elimination of employment discrimination did not become an important priority in the Department of Justice until late in 1967, three years after Congress had passed the law against discrimination in employment. Furthermore, a separate section of lawyers concentrating on Title VII matters, was not established until 1969, under the Nixon Administration.

The Department of Justice filed in February 1966, eight months after the law became effective, but 20 months after it had been passed. The failure to use the one year grace period to plan and prepare for litigation meant that there was that much delay in getting the cases started on their long trial through the court system. One of the purposes of Congress in giving a year's moratorium on the effective date of Title VII was to allow the government to tool up to enforce the laws. This purpose was completely ignored.

By late 1967, two years after the law became effective, but three years after it had been passed, the Department of Justice had filed only eight Title VII cases. They had simply failed to gear up to cope with the problem. In 1968, the number of cases increased, but without an increase in the resources to process them. The result was that the Republican administration inherited a larger case load, but not the neccesary administrative machinery to cope with it.

The department did a good job in some crucial cases which they filed. The most notable are the *Crown Zellerbach case,* where the court of appeals for the Fifth Circuit held that discriminatory seniority systems were illegal; the *Asbestos workers* case which held that union hiring and referral practices were illegal; the *Sheet Metal Workers Local 36* case which dealt with many of the problems of the construction industry discrimination; and the *Hayes Aircraft* case in which the Fifth Circuit ordered the use of preliminary injunctions where the discrimination practices were clear. In some of these cases, notably Crown Zellerbach and Asbestos Workers, the government participated in litigation along with either the NAACP or the Legal Defense Fund, Inc, and attorneys for those organizations are fully entitled to share the credit for these major legal victories. Yet it remains true that they did a good job in the few cases they started. But this is the most that can be said. The massive legal frontal attack against job discrimination which might have come from the Attorney General any time after July 2, 1965, simply never emerged.

B. The EEOC

The second agency reviewed by the U.S. Civil Rights Commission was the Equal Employment Opportunity Commission. I have earlier mentioned some of the problems of the Commission. The most fundamental was that the Commission was given jurisdiction over a huge problem, but without the full support of the President of the United States. At the time the crucial decisions concerning the Commission were made, President Johnson had the election of 1964 and the increasing scope of the Viet Nam conflict on his mind. Nevertheless, the fact remains that he withheld the exercise of the only personal power he had, and this failure to act then affected probably for the worst, everything that happened afterward.

He had one year, from July 2, 1964 until July 2, 1965, to find, and appoint five Commissioners, and for those Commissioners to build a staff and an administrative apparatus so that the Commission could begin to function effectively when the law went into effect. The Commissioners were not appointed until May 10, 1965. At that time, they had less than two months to prepare to enforce the statute. The result was a rush job, and the agency was not able to cope effectively with the masses of complaints which poured in.

The EEOC did adopt some very advanced approaches to enforcement of equal employment opportunity, which might not have

57

developed if the bureaucracy had exercised its usual cautious approach. For example, the concept that the complainant had to agree before a settlement could be reached, was a new approach to enforcement of the law in this field. It followed the approach of Senator Dirkson who had insisted that individual rights must be recognized, rather that have a paternalistic government advising minorities on what was good for them.

Secondly, the concept of a written agreement which specifically altered discriminatory systems of hiring, promotion and seniority was pressed by the Commission beyond its previous development. Prior actions by state agencies and the PCEEO has tended toward pious platitudes but little action. This EEOC concept has been expanded in the current requirements of OFCC Order Number 4, which will discuss later.

Thirdly, the EEOC developed written decisions as to whether there was reasonable cause to believe an employer or union was discriminating. This was important, and helped to lay the foundation for a broad definition of discrimination, a definition which has now been adopted by the Supreme Court of the United States, Fourthly, the Commission issued guidelines to restrict discriminatory use of employment testing—this practice was used to exclude minorities from jobs for reasons which had nothing to do with their ability to do the work required.

Finally, EEOC developed and inplemented the reporting requirements which give us an annual accounting of minority employment. This crucial contribution now produces for us the facts concerning employment patterns which have so influenced our thinking in recent years, in the direction of specific numerical goals, targets and timetables, thus making programs such as the Philadelphia Plan possible.

This is an impressive list of conceptual accomplishments. But the EEOC was not able to bring them into daily action. The overwhelming number of complaints meant that the system was innundated. Massive staff turnover meant that program development— which takes time— never was completed. Lack of budget meant lack of skilled manpower. It is in the area of day to day operations that the Commission floundered. And this, of course, is the precise area where advance planning, in terms of budget, staff and the like, makes a tremendous difference. This weakness is traceable directly back to the delay by President Johnson in appointing the initial set of commissioners.

Later efforts, in 1967-1968 by the Commission, to correct the situation simply made it worse. The backlog at the Commission has made it virtually imposible for that agency to attempt to do anything other than process individual complaints, and the fine plans for ending systems of discrimination throughout the country have not been borne out.

At one point in 1967, the Commission was so intent on clearing up the backlog that it adopted a point system for the investigators. Investigators were given three points for every case they finished. They were expected to get twelve points a month, or to complete four cases. This system was apparently a disaster in terms of the high aspirations of the Commission. The U.S. Civil Rights Commission report says, of the point system:

> Based only on quantity and giving no consideration to quality or case complexity, it proved to be a counter-productive plan, causing, among other confusions, poor quality of performance, administrative closures, the inhibition of broadened charges, and resistance to pursuit of non-alleged violations. (p. 102)

The Commission staff was told to close cases regardless of quality of the work or difficulty of the matter, just to get rid of the backlog. Fortunately, the Commission had adopted a rule which meant that if it did a poor job, the complainant could still go to court, so this did not destroy his legal rights. However, it did delay the day when a complainant could exercise them. Rather than giving the complainant the key to the court house door, the Commission directed the complainant on a long tour before he went to court.

The next chapter will describe efforts by the Commission to improve the situation since 1969. Suffice it to say here, that the "point system" was abolished, and the Commission had decentralized many of its functions to speed up performance. But the dead hand of the backlog still haunts the corridors of the Commission, and limits its ability to take effective regulatory action.

The fact that so many thousands of citizens have filed complainants with the EEOC and continue to do so despite the history of slow performance by that agency is a tribute to the patience and fortitude of America's minority citizens.

C. The Office of Federal Contract Compliance

This agency, the successor to the President's Committee, was formed in 1965 to enforce the anti-discrimination and affirmative action clauses in government contracts. It was to do this by supervising the work of the agencies which purchased goods and services. These agencies were, in turn, to supervise the employment practices of employers who were government contractors. First, the agency was hobbled with a tiny staff—not more than 28 people in 1967—which did not effectively supervise the various purchasing agencies, and, except in the Newport News situation, was unable to effectively control the actions of the major employers. OFCC did not issue its own regulations until 1968, three years after its formation, and when it did so, the regulations were so vague that contractors could go right on discriminating with the excuse that the government had not been specific about what they had to do to avoid discriminating. The various purchasing agencies, notably the Department of Defense, were able to do business as usual with the discriminators, because OFCC did nothing to stop them. OFCC did not develop the data and information necessary to organize an effective and systematic compliance program. It did not consider cancellation or debarment of any contractors until 1968, three years after the agency was created, and at the end of the Johnson administration.

But perhaps the most startling failure of the OFCC reported by the Civil Rights Commission, was its inability to deal with the problem of discrimination in the construction industry. This problem has plagued equal employment opportunity programs from the earliest days and early became the key symbol in the minority community, by which the promises of equal employment opportunities would be measured. Despite this, the OFCC floundered inconclusively, developing different programs in several cities, but implementing none of them in a systematic, orderly way. There was simply a series of improvised approaches to community pressures, each of which was labelled a "plan" with the name of the city attached. These plans were so vague and indefinite, that they did not succeed in influencing the course of discrimination in the trades.

In essence, the report shows that the OFCC from 1965 through 1968 had all the powers to be an effective regulatory agency, but did not use them. It did not give guidance as to what constituted discrimination, nor what steps were required to end it; it did not have systematic enforcement procedures; and it did not establish its credibility by utilizing the sanctions at its command, except, in occasional instances, by delay in issuance of contracts. This was the state of affairs at the end of the Johnson administration —which makes it clear that these inadequacies did not originate with the Nixon administration.

This then is the story of the silent sellout, or how the government which secured the passage of the great Civil Rights Act of 1964, and adopted the tough executive order requiring non-discrimination by government contractors, then failed abysmally in the effectuation of those legal tools to produce equality. The promised land of dignity, equality, work and justice lay within the reach of all Americans but their government did not grasp it.

CHAPTER SEVEN

The Construction Industry 1969-1971

In the years from 1965 to 1968, OFCC had fumbled with a number of ineffective programs in the construction industry. Through this fumbling the organization had begun to develop some ideas of how to do the job of ending discrimination in that industry. The construction industry organized in a way vastly different from most of the economy. The construction industry consists of vast numbers of general and subcontractors who bid on specific jobs. General contractors are rapidly becoming brokers, who bid, but do no work, subcontracting out most or all of the work. Subcontractors, in turn, maintain a small permanent labor force, and, when they obtain a contract, go out to hire the men necessary to perform it. Thus the demand side of the labor market in the construction industry is characterized by sharp peaks and valleys, as contractors hire men for specific jobs, and then fire them when the job is over. In addition, the demand side is further affected by problems of seasonality (not all work can be done in all weather) and the general level of business in the construction industry.

On the supply side, most of the industry is organized by the 19 craft unions which have always represented the workers in the industry. These unions seek exclusive territorial jurisdiction. They seek to control the access to all the jobs in a certain craft in a certain geographical area. If they control these jobs, they can then allocate them to their members and others, thus assuring at least some union members of regular employment, in the face of the fluctuating demand for labor. In addition, by controlling the number of people who come into the trade, they are able to keep the supply of skilled workers at a level which is low enough so that they have strong bargaining power in setting wages with management. The result of this effort, carried on over the years, is that the wage rates in the construction industry are higher than in any other industry. It is important to understand that both the hiring hall, through which the union distributes the jobs, and the decision to restrict the supply of labor are, in themselves, legitimate union objectives, so long as they do not interfere with other, more important values. With such machinery the White-dominated unions have systematically kept Black and Spanish minority workers out of the construction industry.

The NAACP, under the leadership of its fiery director of Labor Relations, Herbert Hill, has focused on the problems of discrimination in construction for nearly two decades, and has made it the central symbol for our time of the quest for equality in employment opportunity. One might argue today that this was a bad choice because the resistance is strongest in this trade, and the payoff in number of jobs is not going to be as great as if, for example, the NAACP had concentrated over the years on a sector of the economic system which was growing more rapidly, such as the white collar area. However, such considerations are not in point, because a decision of twenty years standing has been made that the construction industry is *the* important symbol. This decision, in the context of our pluralism, is the important one which must be recognized and dealt with.

It was in this context that I came into office, early in 1969. In connection with efforts to persuade construction employers to increase minority employment in Cleveland and Philadelphia, the OFCC used "manning tables" in which contractors projected their minority employment needs throughout the course of the job. These manning tables were negotiated between the government and the contractor *after* bids had been awarded. The Comptroller General ruled that this approach was illegal because Federal Contract law requires that the elements of the contract must be specified *before* bids are put out. This decision led the OFCC staff to propose, shortly after I took office, that specific percentage targets for minority employees in several trades, be set forth in Philadelphia and incorporated into the bid specifications in all government contracts issued in that area. OFCC wished to be specific with respect to numbers, and then impose a "good faith" obligation to achieve the numerical results. This was designed to avoid the argument that the numbers constituted "quotas" and hence violated the so-called "no quota" provision of Title VII of the 1964 Civil Rights Act. In fact, one might believe that the opponents of equal opportunity had planned a double play against the compliance program. First, they secured the Comptroller's ruling that the government had to specify exactly the numbers of minorities to be employed, because of the principle that contract specifications must be made clear to bidders before they bid. And then, once the OFCC moved to be specific, the opponents of equal opportunity would claim that the very specificity required under the Comptroller's ruling violated the "no quota" provision of Title VII. The end result was that there was no affirmative action program which was specific enough to have teeth, to advise contractors of their obligations, to assist in increasing minority employment. The government continued to do little in this field, and was criticized by business for not being specific enough.

I don't know if this game plan was fully thought out in circles which opposed our program, but in light of the Comptroller's actions, it certainly looked that way.

At any rate, I decided to go ahead with the Philadelphia Plan of putting specifications of minority employment goals in all contracts. I did this because my study and experience had convinced me that such targets were essential if we are to measure results in terms of increased minority employment. Without such targets, the paper compliance, and the interminable ineffectiveness of the government programs would go on. I had not come to Washington to preside over a continuation of the ineffective programs of the past.

The Secretary backed me. We announced the Philadelphia Plan. The reaction was immediate. The Comptroller ruled that the plan was in violating of the no-quota provision of Title VII and hence illegal.

This precipitated one of the strangest political and constitutional crisis of our generation. First, let us look at the constitutional crisis. The Comptroller is a representative of the Congress who keeps track of expenditures of federal government agencies to make sure that monies appropriated by Congress are spent in accordance with congressional intent. His office in fact certifies that the Treasury Department may pay obligations assumed by the Executive branch. In each agency of government, there is an officer who must certify to the Comptroller that the monies spent by the department have been properly spent.

The Comptroller concerns himself with government contract law and his office renders opinions on many aspects of government contracting. Thus his ruling in 1968 that the manning tables in Philadelphia and Cleveland could not be negotiated after a contract had been signed was fully within his jurisdiction. But his decision in 1969 that the Philadelphia Plan violated the no-quota provision of Title VII was a totally different matter, for he was there interpreting the substance of a federal regulatory statute. He is a representative, not of the courts, or of the Executive, but of the Congress. Had his ruling stood, it would have meant that the Congress could not only pass laws, but interpret them as well. This would have been a radical departure from traditional practices which separate the functions of the various branches of government. Traditionally, Congress passes laws, the Executive carries them out and the courts have the final word on what the law means, and determine whether the Executive stayed within the limits of the law. This concept of the separation of powers lies at the heart of our constitutional system of checks and balances, and the Comptroller's attempt to interpret the laws on behalf of the Congress was a clear and distinct challenge to the principle of separation of powers.

Every government agency has its own lawyers, who interpret for it the meaning of the statute which it is to implement. But the final decision on how any agency in the Executive branch of government may interpret its statute rests not with the agency, but with the chief legal officer in the Executive branch, the Attorney General. Thus, the Comptroller's opposition to the Philadelphia Plan based on an interpretation of Title VII of the Civil Rights Act of 1964, was ultimately an encroachment on the powers of the Attorney General.

The Attorney General, John Mitchell, rose to the challenge and came to the Labor Department for a widely publicized press conference. He came armed with two documents: one, a long and detailed memorandum from the Solicitor or Labor, Lawrence Silberman, arguing that the Philadelphia Plan was legal and did not violate the 'no quota' provisions of the Civil Rights Act, and the other, a shorter opinion of his own, maintaining the same view. Attorney General Mitchell was determined to support the equal employment program which Secretary Shultz and I had developed, both because he believed in it, and because he needed to protect the historic principle of separation of powers. His presentation settled the question of the separation of powers for the time being and the roadblock raised by the Comptroller to the Philadelphia Plan was effectively pushed aside.

If there had been an anti-government strategy of the type I mentioned early, it was thrown off base by this timely intervention by the Attorney General who always responded with vigor and the full support of his office when I needed him to keep the Plan going. However, those who had such a strategy in mind did not give up. Rather, in one of those exciting and unpredictable moves which makes life in Washington fascinating, they shifted the same battle to another forum: the Congress. They did this by having a rider attached to an appropriations bill which would have had the effect of upholding the Comptroller's decision that the Philadelphia Plan was illegal. This would have given the Comptroller general powers to supervise the actions of executive branch agencies, in his decisions with respect to the payment of treasury funds. The rider was to come for a vote in the Senate, and was widely billed as an effort to kill the Philadelphia Plan.

At this point, the President intervened. His Administration was committed to the Philadelphia Plan, and he was himself persuaded that it was a good and workable idea; he was not therefore prepared to have it destroyed in the political arena without a struggle. He publicly and privately placed his political weight against the rider, and began to round up votes in the Senate to kill it. This was his major commitment of the powers of his office, to assist in the carrying out of equal employment opportunity obligations. It was unprecedented for, President Johnson had never intervened to help an agency trying to enforce these laws. But President Nixon was convinced of the importance of the program, and took all the actions he could to see that the rider was defeated.

In the political arena, as the result of presidential intervention, something unprecedented happened. The civil rights movement in the Legislature has long been spearheaded by the "leadership conference," a loose coalition of liberal, labor and civil rights groups, which have stood together to support the passage of the various civil rights laws of the 1960's. This alliance was shattered by the debate on the rider to kill the Philadelphia Plan. Part of labor, of course, supported the rider. George Meany, president of the AFL-CIO comes out of the construction industry, and the constructions unions are very powerful in the massive AFL-CIO institution. But some unions refused to go along with the plan to scuttle the Philadelphia Plan. Thus the united front of labor itself was weakened. But more importantly, the civil rights groups, rather surprised that the President was now the spokesman for the civil rights interests, found that they had to side with the President and against their old friends in labor. Their position contributed to the final outcome, in which the Senate killed the rider, and left the Philadelphia Plan intact. The anti-Philadelphia Plan strategy had backfired for, we could now say that the Senate had, by inference, declared that the Philadelphia Plan was proper.

We inaugurated the Plan in September, 1969. It was immediately taken into court, and a long court battle began. In the end the Courts upheld the Plan.

Meanwhile, on the operational front, the Plan was having difficulties. They stemmed from two sources: first, the old OFCC notion that only government and government-aided construction workers could be covered by a plan. This nonsensical idea was a holdover from the days when the Executive Order had applied only to federal work, and not to all work of federal contractors. This had been changed in the 1961 Executive Order, but the OFCC had not caught up with the change in the construction field. Obviously, compliance with the Executive Order with respect to *all* work is a condition for having a government contract, regardless of how much non-government work an employer has. Thus this limitation in the OFCC thinking was really part of the old failure to enforce the Executive Order.

As long as private construction by government contractors was not covered, they could bunch their minority employees on government work, and thus defeated our objective of increasing minority employment. When we introduced the Washington Plan, in 1970, we covered all work by government contractors, not just government work. Then, in 1971, we amended the Philadelphia Plan to extend it to all work by government contractors, thus eliminating the loop-hole.

But we had great problems in implementing the Plan, because of the OFCC-agency system. The OFCC staff was too small to police the Philadelphia Plan, although our area coordinator, Bennett Stalvey, was largely responsible for its creation. He had to supervise half a dozen government agencies that were financing construction, and the interagency bickering and backbiting which resulted made it difficult to know what was happening in Philadelphia. In addition, another inheritance from the old OFCC days was the failure to have a good information system to keep track of minority participation. In the old government tradition, the OFCC required the submission of great numbers of documents which were simply shelved because there was no one to read them. I ordered a more efficient information developed and we were by 1971, able to monitor compliance with the Philadelphia Plan.

The Plan had become controversial. George Meany still did not like it, and the construction unions grumbled constantly; but it became the symbol of progress in civil rights for the Administration. Other cities pressed for the adoption of the Plan. Anticipating the imposition of several more plans, I delivered a speech in March, 1971 in Washington, D.C. which outraged the President of the Sheetmetal Workers who wrote to President Nixon demanding my resignation. I responded that his union was probably the worst offender against minorities in the country. That ended the exchange.

This speech is reproduced here as Appendix A.

The Philadelphia Plan was instituted in September, 1969. In October, the scene shifted to Chicago, where the two major problems facing America then—discrimination in employment and the war in Viet Nam—had led to violent demonstrations. In the summer of 1969, the black community in Chicago was better organized than anywhere else in the country. They were going to open up the construction industry by force, because the government had failed to do so by law. Waves of violence swept construction sites in the city halting work on projects estimated at some $85 million dollars. Workers carried pistols in their lunch boxes, and the tough Chicago police force came on semi-military duty at construction sites.

The black community asked for our help as their violence was being met by greater violence. We decided to hold hearings in Chicago, with a view to setting up a Philadelphia-type Plan. HUD Assistant Secretary Sam Simmons set up an investigative force and, in late October I went to Chicago with my staff.

It was then a two-ring circus. The trial of the Chicago Seven was just getting under way. The federal court house was under heavy guard, and we could not use it for our hearings. In addition, all the federal police officers, marshalls, FBI agents and the like, were involved in the activities around the Chicago Seven trial. This was to embarrass us later.

The OFCC booked the top floor of a hotel for the hearing. We came into town the day before the hearing, and were interviewed on television. The morning of the hearing, I walked into the room to find it packed with white construction workers. Downstairs, a thousand hard hats picketed. The management of the hotel asked us not to hold the hearing and, in effect, told us to get out, because of the trouble.

I opened the hearing, and took 20 minutes of abuse from the workers assembled there. I then decided we could not go ahead, because they would not let the witnesses into the hearing room, or even into the hotel. The Chicago police were behaving very gently toward the pickets, and would not help us in any way. There was no federal police present.

I recessed the hearing, announcing that it would be reconvened on federal property the next morning. At the same time, I assisted in the distribution of the report which Assistant Secretary Simmons had prepared, based on his investigation. He had been scheduled to read that report, and would do so the following day, but I wanted to be sure that it was given wide publicity, because it represented the most thorough government expose of the problems of discrimination in the trade, and the past failure of government to do anything about it.

I recessed the meeting, and we shouldered our way past some catcalling construction workers. That afternoon, in the hotel, I participated in what must be the strangest meeting of federal officials ever held in Chicago.

The unions had sent word that if the hearing was held the next day they intended to close down construction in Chicago in protest, and picket on a mass basis. They simply wanted the hearing postponed. They had demonstrated their ability to interrupt us on short notice when we were not prepared. Now they were after us in earnest. They wanted the federal government program to get out of Chicago, peacefully if possible, but by mass action if necessary.

Obviously, we faced a crucial challenge. Leonard Garment, the White House Advisor on Civil Rights, and Jerris Leonard, the Assistant Attorney General for Civil Rights, flew in. We sat in that hotel room for several hours discussing whether the federal government could hold a hearing in Chicago on the problem of the construction industry. The problem was two-fold: finding a site, since the federal building was occupied with the trial of the Chicago Seven and, providing security of access for witnesses and the public, against the anticipated mass picketing by the construction workers. The site problem was solved by selecting the U.S. Customs Court House, which was downtown, but stood isolated on a block away from heavy trafic. The concern for the mass picketing was not so easily handled. There were no available federal police to handle it, and the Chicago police were obviously siding with the hard hats.

But the inevitable decision was made: the federal government had to demostrate that it could function in Chicago. The full hearing had to be held, if there was to be anything left of the federal anti-discrimination program. The White House advised us that it was prepared to either mobilize the National Guard, or airlift troops to the city if that was necessary in order to see that the hearing was held.

And so here in Chicago, fresh from our confrontation with the legal-political process over the Philadelphia Plan, we faced the elementary forces of life, racism and fear of loss of jobs, and another constitutional test: this one of naked power. In our constitutional system, a hearing is considered either essential or desirable, before significant government action is taken. If the government could not hold a hearing, it was helpless to do anything meaningful. (Note the converse is not true: the simple fact that we held a hearing did not necessarily mean that we would do anything meaningful.) But the apparent helplessness of the federal government would destroy not only all the EEO program, but many other programs as well. It could not be that a mass of hard hats could stop the federal government from functioning. If the test was to come through the application of force, then the troops who had been on riot duty in 1967 and 1968 would come to Chicago and deal with the situation.

Once the decisions were made, I tried to relax. But the FBI had picked up a rumor of a threat of physical violence. My staff and I were packed abruptly out of the hotel, and we spent the night in another place, with armed guards sitting in the corridor outside our rooms.

The next morning, I hailed a cab to go to the hearing, accompanied by Horace Monasco, Alex Poinsett, the Ebony reporter, and Al Blumrosen, my consultant. Fortunately for all of us, I sat on the left side of the cab. When we reached the Court House, it was surrounded by thousands of hard hats who simply blocked off all the regular accesses to the building. As we stood in the stalled traffic, men kept walking by and scanning the occupants of the cars. They were looking for me, and they knew what I looked like from the television interviews. But because I was on the far side of the car from the curb, I was not recognized. (Later, another tall black man who was coming to testify was roughed up on his way to the hearing. He had been mistaken for me.) We found a back entrance which was not blocked by pickets, and got out of the cab. I was at once spotted, and followed into the building by catcalls and obscenities.

The Chicago police did nothing for two hours to provide access to the building through the crowd of hard hats. Finally, a seires of compromises began and witnesses were allowed in. Assistant Secretary Simmons testified, and we were underway.

The next day, the hard hats were there, but orderly, and the police saw to it that access to the federal building was blocked to the public. I believe the threat of federal troops, plus the risk of a wild confrontation between the white workers and an aroused black community, led to the local officials to decide to enforce the law.

The immediate result of the hearing was that the contractors and the unions, under pressure from the mayor, agreed to negotiate with the black coalition concerning increases in minority employment opportunity. While we had the evidence to justify the setting up of a Plan, we did not do so. However, we did issue notices which had the effect of preventing 17 contractors from securing any more government contracts until they had submitted an acceptable affirmative action plan.

The HUD area equal opportunity officer, Robert Tucker, along with my consultant, Al Blumrosen, began to assist in the negotiations, advising the minority community behind the scenes. This was clearly the moment for a major breakthrough. The black community had everything going for it: good organization, the ability to take to the streets and demonstrate physical power and also, the fact that the government was on their side, with all of the leverage which the contract program could give. It should have been an auspicious breakthrough. Instead, it was a disastrous failure.

Tucker and Blumrosen were called off. The Black coalition thereafter negotiated an agreement which was weak, but once they had done so, we could not impose a Philadelphia-type Plan. Worst of all, we were committed by the Secretary of Labor, to maximum support for the concept of the "home town solution" to problems of discrimination in the construction industry. This meant that we would encourage negotiations between the black community, contractors and unions across the country, aimed at adopting programs to increase minority participation in the construction trades. We were good soldiers fighting for a lost cause. We developed a model agreement to be used because the minority community did not have the technical resources to conduct negotiations against the skilled lawyers and negotiators of labor and management. Our area coordinators worked unceasingly to help the minority communities pull themselves together for these negotiations. The result was two years lost, a long series of futile and fruitless negotiations, no really successful Plans, and a new and deeper level of bitterness in the black community.

By the end of 1969, we had the two competing models for dealing with the discriminatory patterns in the construction industry: the Philadelphia Plan and the "home town solutions." Through 1970 and into 1971, we proceeded in both directions at once. We promoted home town solutions, and held hearings with the aim of introducing Plans in Newark, St. Louis, Washington (where we did actually set a plan), Atlanta, San Francisco and Los Angeles. But the hearings were not meaningful as, time after time, the introduction of further Plans was delayed. Finally, in the spring of 1971, the delay became personally intolerable to me. And I directed the preparation of the action memorandum which I will discuss in the next chapter. Meanwhile, as we struggled with these problems on a city by city basis, we began to conceive of a national plan covering the entire country. I put my staff and my consultant to work developing the plan. The key was a procedure to set goals and targets for every county in the nation, based on a survey of the nationwide pattern of discrimination.

The Rutgers Law School research project under the direction of Al Blumrosen produced the concept which made it possible to develop the national plan. The concept is that if the construction industry had not engaged in systematic discrimination against minorities, it is fair to assume that the minority participation in that industry would be roughly the same as minority participation at similar skill levels, in the rest of industry in the locality. Thus the proportion of skilled and semi-skilled minority workers in the non-construction sector of industry became the goal for minority participation in construction. And this figure was available from government computers because employers in the rest of industry have been filing reports on the racial and ethnic composition of their work force. Once this concept was understood, it became feasible to adopt goals for every county in the nation, which would be solidly based on the experience of the rest of industry in the area.

When this concept evolved, we moved as quickly as possible toward the concept of a national plan. And so, in the summer of 1971, we sat poised to solve the problem of discrimination in the construction trades. Our tools were developed and sharpened through the toughening process which we have described: on the streets of Chicago, in the cloak room of the United States Senate, at conference tables in the White House, in the black community organizations, in the courts and on the job sities. We were, finally, ready to do the job.

The text of a speech I delivered in Chicago in the Spring of 1971 appears as Appendix B.

CHAPTER EIGHT

Tooling Up the Rest
of the OFCC Program

The shambles I inherited called OFCC required a stem-to-stern reorganization. John Wilks began at the beginning, and in two years, had done all the things necessary to get OFCC internally into shape to do its job. For example, he straightened out the confusing question of what government agency supervised what employer, by assigning employers in various industries to specific agencies. Before that, it had not been clear to either the agencies or the employers who was in charge.

Secondly, he brought in new people, with new ideas to develop a systematic approach to discrimination. Computer and personnel specialists began to organize compliance reviews so that they could be effective. His staff and consultants revised regulations to make it clear that OFCC had the authority to direct the other agencies, and made it clear for the first time that the minority workers were entitled to full participation in the compliance re- view program. No longer was the compliance to consist of private talks between the government representative and the employer; the employees were to become a party to the compliance review process, and were to be advised of its results.

The staff and consultants developed not only specific guidelines as to what was appropriate, affirmative action but also specific in- terpretations of what constituted discrimination. Model affirma- tive action plans were prepared, as were guidelines dealing with the vexing problems of religious and ethnic discrimination. The testing guidelines were revised. Of all of this flurry of activity only one product, Order Number 4, requiring detailed affirmative action plans by employers was released by the Department. This became the basis for compliance programs. Order Number 4 was important, but was only the beginning of a total revision of the compliance review concept with a view to make it an effective law enforcement tool. We had done our work, but the bureaucracy did not release its results.

Meanwhile, we increased our staff from 28 and reorganized internally. By the spring of 1971, I could say that we were ready, not only in the field of construction, but also in the rest of our area of responsibility, to become an effective law enforcement agency. We were prepared to act so as to gain the respect of other agencies, and of employers and unions, and to develop the credibility which had long been lost, among the minority community. But crisis after crisis intervened in the Labor Department, and our energies seemed to be drained away. We were becoming another typically inactive agency, more concerned about our internal affairs, because we suffered the frustration of not being able to implement our program. With all our effort, we seemed to be slipping into the very pattern of inaction which I was determined to avoid, and which had, over the years, prevented the program from functioning. Some of the problems were within the Department of Labor, while others required political decision from the White House.

Our programs—the national plan for the construction industry and the specific technical procedures necessary to make the compliance program work in the rest of industry—were stalled at various points in the bureaucracy in the spring of 1971. The memorandum which I had prepared was to serve as the basis for springing them loose, and putting them into effect. At this moment (May, 1971) I do not know whether my list will be fully acted upon. Meanwhile, cross currents which characterize the nation's capital and daze those concerned with making government work, swirl around our work at OFCC. A few examples are set out below.

The "hometown solution" in the construction industry was triggered off by the Chicago Plan. In May 1971, an alderman of the City who was in charge of administering training funds under the Chicago Plan, was wanted in connection with forgery of checks drawn on the training money. There was the possibility that this might cast doubt on the validity of the hometown solution and thus strengthen my efforts to secure imposed plans, and a national plan.

From around the country, hometown plans were failing, and a demand was growing for the imposition of Philadelphia-type plans, in Pittsburgh and Denver, to mention only two.

The U.S. Civil Rights Commission began to seriously monitor enforcement activities in the Civil Rights field. It scheduled hearings with senior administrators for June. This was intended to trigger off more intensive enforcement action.

The Black Caucus of Congressmen, having met with the President in March, secured a response in May. The response cited the record of performance in the field of jobs discrimination as a strong part of the Administration program.

Congress was clearly considering transferring OFCC to the EEOC. Supporters of the move were motivated, in part, by a desire to get the program removed from my office.

Within the Labor Department, bureaucratic maneuvers continued to attempt to restrict my authority.

The pressures from unions in the construction industry for my resignation continued to mount.

The day-to-day frustrations of the bureaucratic process in Washington, the constant bustling of speaking engagements, meetings and conferences around the country were taking their toll of my physical strength. As the Spring wore on, and the elements of my program remained stalled at various points in the process, I more and more seriously wondered whether we could, in fact, get ourselves together within the Government to do the job of enforcing the equal employment laws.

For I viewed all of these activities within the context of my own program for the 1970's. Shortly after I took office, I had prepared a comprehensive program to make economic parity for minorities by 1980, a national goal, on the same order of priority as the decision to go to the moon. I had submitted the program to the White House, and had received no response: Elements of the program are spelled out in Appendix C. And, although the plan was not accepted, it remained my personal framework of action, giving me strength to continue the day-to-day efforts. But if the time should come when I conclude that these efforts are fruitless, and that the goal of law enforcement cannot be achieved, and that the larger goal of economic parity for minorities by 1980 is too evanascent a dream to pursue, then I would have to close this chapter of my life. As I reflect on the last two exciting and frustrating years, I cannot identify a single cause for all of our difficulties, or a single reason for our successes. I feel that I have wrestling with the evil giant of racism in a variety of its forms: overt, covert and unconscious.

Of all these forms, perhaps the unconscious forms are the most difficult to battle. And in the battle, I saw growing hatred, bitterness, alienation and that division of America into two lands by race, which the Kerner Commission feared after the 1967 riots. And I saw the great hope fade from our grasp.

But I have been sustained by my faith thus far, that we have no alternative but to try to make our dreams real.

At the end of May, 1971 I was asked to address the Annual convocation of the Presbyterian Church of the United States on the subject of racism and repression.

This gave me an opportunity to sum up my frustration over the battle against discrimination, and to focus on the one event which will sustain my efforts for a little time more. This event was the decision of the Supreme Court, written by Chief Justice Burger, in *Griggs v. Duke Power Co.,* which I discussed earlier. Griggs gave new hope. It seemed to me that in some very profound way, the black and other minorities in America, indeed, did believe in law and order, and, finally, on the judgment of the Supreme Court, as to the direction that America would take.

More than 100 years ago, the French observer, Toqueville, noticed that we Americans used law far more than Europeans to solve our problems. It has been a characteristic of America since the earliest times, and remains true today. And so, when I read *Griggs v. Duke Power* against the background of my frustrations concerning the enforcement and implementation of the anti-discrimination principle, I was encouraged to go on. For the court not only understood discrimination, it defined it in terms so clear and stark that enforcement programs could not but help to be improved. In *Griggs,* the company had used a high school degree requirement, and certain tests which were not job-related, to select its personnel. The result was that many qualified individuals from minorities were screened out and denied promotional opportunities. The Supreme Court held that these employer actions were illegal under Title VII of the Civil Rights Act of 1964, and the EEOC guidelines concerning the discriminatory use of employment testing were to be enforced.

It was against that background, in the light of the entire two years of experience with the battle against discrimination, that I spoke to the Presbyterian Assembly on the nature of racism in America. The speech appears as Appendix D.

In the summer of 1971, I felt that I had brought the OFCC to the brink of effectiveness. At that point, the President suggested that I should move to a larger stage—the United Nations. From there, I believed I might get into another position from which I could see more of my ideas through to fruition. I accepted the challenge and resigned as Assistant Secretary of Labor. I felt I could do no more where I was, and it was time to seek another way to carry forward the quest for justice and dignity.

CHAPTER NINE

How To Get the Job Done

We have developed the technical tools to enforce the Executive Order. Never before has this been true. We have tooled up as far as it is possible to do so. Yet, our programs are stalled at various points within government. These other units in government are not racist. They simply have other things to do, and do not place the emphasis on solving the problems of employment discrimination. Meanwhile, civil rights organizations and leaders hurl a mounting wave of criticism at the administration for its inaction. Rather than helping to get the job done, they appear content to criticize from the side lines. In this, I think they are naive about the nature of the American governmental process.

They believe that once a law is passed, it will be automatically implemented. This is not so. When they see that the laws are not being implemented, they direct their criticism at the administrator, and feel they have done all that is possible.

They have taken the concept of separation of powers too seriously. They think that once Congress has acted to pass a law, or the President has promulgated an executive order, that these will be carried out automatically. This is not the nature of our government. They have confused the important constitutional principle of separation of powers with the way the governmental process actually operates. To clarify thinking, we must understand that there is a single governmental process involved in passing and implementing a law or executive order. In this single process, the action may shift from time to time to different participants: the Congress, the President, the Courts, the independent agencies, or the cabinet agencies. Those who are skilled in the governmental process know this, and do not hesitate to shift from one forum to another to get things done. They apply full pressure at each point, until their program is a success. Recall the way that the construction industry fought against the Philadelphia Plan, using the Courts, the Congress and the controller general.

The secret of success then, is in the application of constant and maximum political pressure at every stage in a program, from passage on legislation until that legislation is implemented. But the Civil Rights community wants to rest on its laurels once it has secured the passage of a law. They do not lobby day in and day out to help civil rights agencies get bigger budgets, or see to it that good and effective men are appointed to office, or that the rules and regulations of a program are designed to make it work properly, or that programs are designed and implemented in such a way as to carry out the objectives of the civil rights movement.

Good intentioned administrators alone cannot do this job. The reason is that the other side is constantly present, pressing their views on how things ought to be done. Unless the civil rights interests are represented persistently in the constant administrative infighting, their views will not prevail. So, the civil rights activists should be working with friendly administrators in government, not against them. And they must become involved in the technical details of programs and plans to see that they operate fairly.

Let me give one illustration which will show most of my concern. The basic procedure used by OFCC to enforce the Executive Order in most of industry is called a compliance review. Under Order No. 4, the contractor prepares an analysis of his problems of race, ethnic origin, religion and sex discrimination. This analysis is reviewed by a compliance officer who either approves of the plan or suggests and negotiates changes in it. In a few cases of recalcitrant employers, or when there is some external reason for publicity, the matter may go toward formal hearings. But in 99% of the cases, the *only* proceeding is this informal compliance review. The result of this review is that the contractor is permitted to receive government contracts.

Traditionally, the affirmative action plans and the compliance review documents have been kept confidential between the government and the contractor. Minority workers, and organizations representing minority persons have never had access to the plans and the reviews, even though the plans and reviews determine the rights of minority persons under the Executive Order and under the Civil Rights Act of 1964. This confidentiality has meant that, from the perspective of minority interests, the government official on the site and the contractor could make an arrangement which would settle the rights of minority workers, and permit a contractor to receive contracts, without any required participation and reviews by the workers or their representatives. I consider this a shocking denial of essential elements of fairness and due process to the workers, and have proposed for more than a year a change in our regulations which will correct this situation.

This is most important for practical reasons. The only effective review of the fairness of an affirmative action plan must involve the workers. Otherwise, the compliance officers will write reports which make their work look good, and they may be unaware of some facts concerning discrimination. Thus, internal paper reviews conducted by OFCC supervising the compliance agencies are inherently of limited validity. The minority workers must have a part in enforcing the Executive Order or it will never work properly.

My proposed reform has been stalled. Management argues against it, on the grounds that certain confidential information is disclosed during these reviews which they are entitled to keep secret. This argument, if it prevails, will permit the compliance process to continue to be one essentially between the contractor and the government, to the disadvantage of the minority workers.

At this point, it is absolutely essential that there be counter political influence brought to bear by the minority and civil rights interests. Otherwise, the management view will prevail. This pressure could be brought to bear through lobbyists, through pressures from black congressmen, through newspaper stories, through speeches, or perhaps, through a lawsuit under the Freedom of Information Act. The point is not the tactics of pressure, but the importance of using it, at this key point in the administrative process.

Up to now, such precisely applied pressures have not been used by the Civil Rights movement. The spokesmen have not concerned themselves with the details of administration and have fought for programs which will be fair to minorities. At the moment, the key issue, I believe, is the one I mentioned above, but next month and next year, these issues will change. At each point, labor, management, and others will exert maximum pressure. Unless the Civil Rights interest is also pressed, it will lose.

For the American Government is one continuous process from legislation to implementation. Unless the Civil Rights movement is prepared to constantly press for effective implementation, to demand effective, technically adequate programs, the gains in Congress can be cancelled in administration. Merely criticizing the Administration is not enough. The Civil Rights movement must be present and vocal on precise, technical issues day in and day out. Thus far, the movement has simply not undertaken this task. Until it does so, the best mentioned administrators will have their hands tied in the gossamer strings of bureaucracy.

With effective day-to-day pressure from the Civil Rights movement, on the other hand, many of these difficult barriers can be overcome by tough-minded administration. In the Newport News case, for example, the Civil Rights community was present through the entire proceedings, for the fact that the NAACP had filed a lawsuit against the company.

For the Civil Rights interests to prevail in the face of this opposition, it is not enough for us to be right. We must also be on top of each issue at each point where the implementation of our laws could be frustrated. This is an art which the Civil Rights movement has not yet developed. Until it does so, it will not realize its full potential, and well-intentioned administrators will achieve less than the maximum possible enforcement of the laws.

While the Constitution vests in the President the duty to see that the laws are faithfully executed, the power to assure that this is done fully rests with the people.

The Old Order Is Collapsing

Speech Delivered to the Annual Meeting and Legislative Conference of the Associated Builders and Contractors Inc., Washington, D. C., March 12, 1971

Ladies and gentlemen, I am pleased to be here today, for a very special reason. In every speech I have given since becoming assistant secretary of labor, I have had to marshall and present the arguments for the adoption of an equal opportunity program —particuarly in construction—by government, contractors and unions. I have explained at great length, the dreary figures with which you are so familiar—the double unemployment rate of minorities, the quadruple teenage minority unemployment rate. I have explained the nature of discrimination in our society, discrimination which had been identified time and time again in court decisions, and in hearings which I have held or directed in connection with the problems of the construction industry. Long before the "hard hats" surfaced resulting from the violent confrontation with students in New York City, the hard hats also tried to prevent me from holding such a hearing in Chicago. This was back in the fall of 1969.

But today I am making no such argument, I am making no such explanation of the problems. Rather I am here to announce what is already a fact.

The old order is not only under pressure to change: the old

order is collapsing. The institutional systems which have supported invidious racial discrimination in the construction industry are being destroyed. The era of arrogance and discrimination by some unions has ended. Corrupted by their sense of power, they have overreached. And the institutional systems which they built up, turned out to rest on sand, not rock. We are within a year of a great influx of minority workers into the construction trades, as the citadel of labor supply control plus overt discrimination is being destroyed. When this influx comes, you will have a great responsibility. I want to talk about your responsibility: but first, I want to explain my announcement to you that the era of union domination of the employment pattern in the construction industry is over.

The first point I want to make concerns the nature of employment in the construction industry. I need not belabor that with you. You know of the hiring halls, the exclusive referral arrangements and, more importantly, of the principle that no man works without union approval. You also know that, particularly in the metal trades, unions have over the years excluded blacks and other minorities, including white if they didn't have relatives belonging to the trade. Therefore you knew that when you contract with a union to supply your labor, you are virtually assuring in many instances, that you will receive a substantially all white labor force, whatever the promises may be which you have made with the office of Federal Contract Compliance. Your basic argument has been that you were required, by virtue of the collective bargaining relations with your unions, to adopt and assist in the implementation of the segregated pattern of union membership and referral to work.

What I have to say is against the background of your understanding of your situation. It is this. The union grip on the processes of government has been weakened considerably if not broken. The union movement was not able to kill off the Philadelphia Plan inside the Labor Department, it was not able to head off the Philadelphia Plan before the Attorney General. The union was not able to beat the Philadelphia Plan in the Congress. The President, the Attorney General and others rallied behind it. The unions were whipped. Why? Is it because the Philadelphia Plan is so intrinsically sound? I don't think so. We have had many problems with the plan, and the bugs are not out of it yet. But the Plan has survived all of these attacks because it is the symbol of an intention on the part of the government, for the first time in a 30-year history of these programs, to effectively and meaningfully enforce the anti-discrimination laws.

The President saw it that way; so did the Attorney General, and so did the federal judge in Philadelphia. Let me quote from his opinion:

> In retrospect, it is the court's belief that the denial of equal employment opportunity must be eliminated from our society..It is beyond question, that present employment practices have fostered and perpetuated a system that has effectively maintained a segregated class. That concept, if I may use the strong language it deserves, is repugnant, unworthy, and contrary to present national policy. The Philadelphia Plan will provide an unpolluted breath of fresh air to ventilate this unpalatable situation. Justice demands an end to all artifices that prevent one, who because of color is stopped from enjoying the same opportunities that are accorded to those of different color. The destiny of minority group employment is the primary issue and the Philadelphia Plan will provide an equitable solution to this troublesome problem.

This is the mood of the courts—not only of the court in Philadelphia, but of the Fifth Circuit Court of Appeals, which upheld an order requiring a union to scrap its referral system and hiring hall procedures, and refer one white and one black alternately (U.S. v. Asbestos Workers). It is the mood of the Federal District Court in Seattle which required the "sacred cow" apprenticeship program of the ironworkers to contain twenty-five percent minority workers, or seven, whichever was greater. And it is the mood of the Federal Court in Newark which upheld the Newark Medical School plan during the last month. In addition, several other courts that have spoken, have found discrimination in the construction trades, and have issued orders which have a breadth and sweep which make it clear that the courts do not intend to allow a continuation of discrimination.

And so we have, for the first time in our history, a President and an Attorney General who support a specific anti-discrimination program in this field, and a court system which will uphold this program. Now, for the first time, we have the opportunity to take effective action to end the strangle hold on these jobs in certain of the lily white construction craft unions. The ball is in our corner. What have we done with it? Let's look at the record.

When I came into office, The Office of Federal Contract Compliance was a moribund agency. It now has 96 employees, and is beginning to exercise its function of giving orders to the various compliance agencies and its developing policies. The Philadelphia Plan and The Washington Plan are two illustrations of the capability of OFCC in this area. The Plans may not be perfect, but they represent an advance over the previous period of incompetent, soft administration of the Office of Federal Contract Compliance.

When I came into office, the unions dominated The Apprenticeship Approval Program in The Bureau of Apprenticeship and Training. B.A.T. had issued regulations concerning Equal Opportunity in Apprenticeship Programs which were not meant to be taken seriously. New regulations have just been issued which require unions that segregate to adopt goals and timetables to introduce minorities into the apprenticeship programs.

Previously, on-the-job training programs would not be funded by the labor department without union approval. Under new regulations, such approval is no longer necessary.

And where unions were relying on The Davis-Bacon Act to eliminate non-union competition they are no longer doing so.

Finally, the union movement in the construction industry thought it could control The Congress, The Courts and The President. It has been demonstrated since, that not only do they not control these institutions, but their practices of discrimination make all of their institutions very vulnerable. They have lost public support because of the outrageous abuse of their power, both in terms of demands for heavy wage increases, and in the effort which they have made to preserve the segregated character of some of the unions.

And that is why I am here to announce the end of the era.— The end of the era of union dominance in the construction industry.

All around the country, unions, management representatives and representatives of the black community are sitting down at conference tables trying to work out hometown solutions to these problems. Two years ago, there would have been no such meetings. Today, such meetings may be fruitful, but they may be too late. For it is perfectly clear that the only thing that counts now is results; and that without such results, we shall impose plan after plan in cities where the hometown solution doesn't work, until we move toward the concept of a nationwide plan. We will continue to root out discrimination practices by the unions. We will do this by introducing many more blacks and Spanish workers into the trades. The craft unions no longer have the power—in court, in Congress, or with The President—to stop such a plan.

Now that it is evident that changes have been made regarding The Federal Government's attitude on fair employment and government contractors, what must you do as a contractor to help us succeed?

First, you must develop result-oriented affirmative programs. Then you must do all you can to get minority group workers and trainees to accept your offer of employment and on-the-job training type placement opportunities. You must also recognize that certain craft unions, plus others, will attempt to prevent you from fulfilling your affirmative action commitments. If and when this happens, file a formal complaint with The Office of Federal Contract Compliance, and we will institute the necessary legal action to remedy this situation forthwith.

Secondly, when you hire more black and Spanish Americans, you have an opportunity to demonstrate that the long apprentice programs in many of these trades is a farce. You can train and educate these minority workers to become journeymen in very little time. The risk is that you will consider such people as simply cheap labor, and not assist them to move up. I warn you seriously against this course. Too often in history black people have been used as strike breakers, only to be put aside by management, and discriminated against by employers, when they had served the purpose of breaking the union. I want to make clear to you that this new era, which will see the black and Spanish American in his rightful place in the construction workforce, will not repeat those mistakes of the past. And it is your responsibility to see that the civil rights movement is not perverted into an anti-labor, anti-worker movement.

You will, in the next few years, be hiring many more minority workers. Many of them will come in as trainees, or advanced trainees—men with some experience or capability, but not at the journeyman level. You will hire many black and Spanish laborers, who have in fact worked in the various trades, without ever getting credit for it, either in terms of money or position. If you view them as a source of cheap labor, you will keep them at the semi-skilled level. But if you view them as upwardly mobile Americans, who have been recently liberated from the bondage that is the heritage from slavery, then you will in fact see that they get the broad experience and the broad training which will equip them to become journeymen. We will insist that this be done in our rules and regulations, but you know as well as I, that the extent to which these regulations are complied with is more a function of your willingness to comply, than of our ability to force you to do so.. Of course we will bring test cases of contractors beginning to exploit the civil rights movement as a source of cheap labor. But that is not the solution. The solution is for you to take your responsibilities seriously to both recruit and hire, and upgrade and train these minorities so that they will become the next generation's craftsmen. That is the responsibility I leave you with.

As for the government, I can say confidently that this new era—the new apprentice regulation, the New OJT regulations, the suspension of Davis Bacon, the upholding of the Philadelphia and Newark plans, the pressure for hometown solutions, coupled with the willingness to impose as broad a set of plans as the national interest requires—will not end. The Courts and The Executive are of one mind on the point made by the judge in The Philadelphia Plan Case which I quoted earlier. Furthermore, The Internal Improvements in the operation of the Office of Federal Contract Compliance mean that our ability to respond to and deal with these problems is improving daily. I would be less than candid with you if I did not admit that at times the department has responded to problems of discrimination in a sluggish manner, if at all. But those days are gone. Our enlarged staff, better trained and operating under a clearer mandate, means that we have, or are in the process of developing, the full capability necessary to insure a national solution to a problem which is national in scope.

My office has held hearings in Newark, Chicago, St. Louis, San Francisco, and Washington, D.C. We have, as a result, imposed and supported plans in Newark, Philadelphia, and Washington. The Federal Courts have found union discrimination in Indiana, Ohio, Washington State, Missouri, and Louisiana. The EEO statistics demonstrate that some of the trades segregate, still, on a nation wide basis. The pattern of discrimination is national.

Therefore, the response of government must, and will be, as broad and as deep as is necessary to meet the full scope of the problem. If you do your part, I can assure you that we will do ours. Between us, we can rid the nation of this heritage of slavery, and get about the important business of life in a republic where men and women are equal as a matter of economic fact, as well as in law.

Thank you.

National Goals for the Construction Industry

The Electrical World Executive Conference
Chicago, Illinois, May 13, 1971

Those of us who have worked over the years to improve minority employment opportunities have often argued that such programs would be good for the nation, not merely good for minorities. The subject of this conference is a vivid demonstration of that proposition, although it gives me no great pleasure to be able to say "we told you so."

This conference is made necessary by the practices of the skilled trades unions in limiting their membership, so as to keep the supply of labor small, and the price high. Both high prices and small supply now threaten not only the private interests of commercial developers, but the public interest in having an adequate supply of electric power. There are other public interests threatened, too, by this situation. The American housing production process is simply producing the decent, safe, suitable housing for all Americans which was established as a national goal in 1949. Our public buildings and private institutions all suffer under the incredible tribute which the skilled building trades demand. Now it may be that the trade union tactics of limiting the supply of labor to keep the price high are, in the abstract, fully legitimate. It is certainly clear that, without union protection, employers would tend to exploit the maximum of labor at the lowest price.

Therefore, I want it clearly understood that I am not attacking—indeed I support—trade union policies which are aimed at protecting the legitimate interests of all workers.

However, the trade union policies of most of the skilled building trades do not fall into that classification. They did not limit the size of the skilled labor force in order to benefit all workers, but only those whites who got into the trades, and their friends and families. The result is that blacks and Spanish workers have been excluded from these good jobs. By excluding the black labor force, the building trades unions of which I speak have kept down the supply of labor, and the price has been kept up. In part, the high price of skilled construction labor may be measured by the exclusion of blacks and other minorities from the trades. If blacks and other minorities were present in the skilled construction trades in the same proportion as they exist in the rest of industry, the construction industry labor force would be considerably larger than it is today, and many of the problems you are struggling with would appear in a totally different context.

Taking the skilled construction trades, for example, the following unions reflect very low percentages of black and Spanish workers:

Boilermakers	9	Percent
Electrical workers	5	"
Elevator Constructors	3	"
Iron Workers	5	"
Plumbers and Pipefitters	2.4	"
Sheetmetal Workers	5	"

The overall minority participation rate in the above trades is 1.6 black, and 3.2 Spanish Americans. Most work in the skilled trades falls into the classification of craftsmen and journeymen work on the one hand, and "operatives" or semi-skilled work on the other. Apprentices and trainees are considered as operatives. Now, if the skilled trades listed above had achieved the same proportion of minority employment as the rest of industry in connection with minority craftsmen and operatives, the labor supply picture would look very different. Nationally, based on

EE-I reports filed by employers largely in the nonconstruction sector of the economy, black and Spanish workers accounted for approximately 12 percent of the operatives and craftsmen in the nation, in nonconstruction work. In the more populous areas, the percentages are strikingly higher. In Illinois, for example, black and Spanish craftsmen and operatives constitute 22 percent of all craftsmen and operatives. Yet in the group of skilled trades with which we are concerned, they constitute less than five percent. This is the case, for example, with respect to the Mexican-American participation in the construction trades in Phoenix, Arizona. Under these circumstances, minority participation would vary, depending on a variety of factors, and could reach a high 20 percent in those states where minorities are heavily represented in the work force. Now, it would be foreign to our traditions to squeeze out of the workforce, minority workers come into it, albeit under discriminatory circumstances. Therefore, it seems to me that we must increase the size of the work-force to permit minority employment in construction to rise roughly to the levels of minority employment in the rest of industry. This would mean, in the populous states—with heavy minority participation in the labor force—an increase of some 20 percent in the skilled and semi-skilled categories in the trades we are concerned with. I think the manpower implications of such an increase are clear.

I conclude, that the price you pay for the discriminatory practices in the construction trades is that, in the populous states, the construction labor force is some 15 percent smaller that it would be if the unions —with the assistance of the contractors—were not permitted to continue their practices of discrimination and exclusion. If you are looking for a source of increased supply of skilled workers, and you are wondering how to bring labor costs under some rational system, I think it would be possible for the Department of Labor to compute the percentages of minority employment which would exist in construction industry in each county in the nation if that industry had the same pattern of minority employment in skilled and semi-skilled workers as the rest of industry. This capability exists because of the operation of the reporting forms EEO-1. An outline of some of the results from such a study is attached.

Thus it would be possible to derive minority employment goals for the skilled trades in the construction industry for each county in the nation, based on the experience of the rest of industry. To then adopt such goals as targets by which to measure performance in the construction industry would, I think, be a relatively simple matter. Lawyers talk about how the law requires all of us to measure up to the standard of the reasonable man. The reasonable man is often, though not always, the average man. Certainly what most of industry does by way of minority employment, when not discriminating, makes a reasonable target to aim at. We know that such a target is attainable, because the rest of industry has attained it. I do not suggest that all skilled and semi-skilled work is interchangeable by any means, and I know that not all those listed as craftsmen in the EEO-1 data would perform in construction. Nevertheless, as a general target, the figure is a realistic and comfortable one to work with.

I would not make this suggestion with respect to white collar employment where the hiring practices of industry in general have been, in my view, discriminatory. Nor does this proposal suggest that there is no discrimination in hiring and placement of employees in the nonconstruction sector of the economy. This is not the case. Nevertheless, the performance record of the rest of industry is so much better than that of the construction industry with respect to skilled and semi-skilled workers, that it is fair and appropriate to use their performance as a benchmark for the construction industry.

Now, the occupation distribution of craftsmen and operatives is different in most of industry and construction. In construction, you use roughly one semi-skilled worker for every two skilled workers, while in the rest of industry, the ratio is one skilled to four semi-skilled. But it seems to me that this demonstrates that the construction industry has a potential for expanded use of semi-skilled workers. This is precisely the level at which many minority workers would come into the trade, and therefore, the civil rights interests, and your interests exactly coincide at that point.

I have shared with you my thinking about how the problems confronting your industry, and the problems confronting minorities in their quest for equal employment opportunity coincide. We may need to develop a pattern of national goals, in the government to make it possible for you to supply adequate electrical energy for the country. We may need to do so, because it is the only effective way, to end employment discrimination. Our activities in this area have been encouraged as a result of the decision of the Third Circuit Court in upholding the Philadelphia Plan, and the decision of the Supreme Court of the United States, holding that discrimination it to be measured by the consequences to minority employment, not by the intention of the employer.

I came to this city a year and a half ago to hold the first of our hearings on the problems of minority employment in construction, I heard the story here, and then the same story many times elsewhere in the nation. It is a story of discriminatory policies, and of informal efforts to negotiate settlements which have almost uniformly failed. I now believe, on the basis of a nationwide examination of the problem, that only a nationwide solution to the problem will give us a chance to do that which is both right and economically desirable. I think the time has come to think about nationwide goals, for minority participation in the skilled trades based on the experience of the rest of industry in each locality in hiring and retaining skilled and semi-skilled minority employees. If the time comes when such goals are forthcoming, I hope we can count on your open support for such programs. For I think this discussion has demonstrated a genuine community of interest which is rarely recognized, between the groups you represent and the minority community. The civil rights battle is often a lonely one.

Now, I realize that an influx of 15 to 20 percent of employees into the skilled trades in the immediate future will create unprecedented problems of education and training which will overwhelm the traditional modes of training and will require new concepts and organization. Some of these concepts are already established as a result of the civil rights efforts, for example, the concept of a short program of instruction for "advanced trainees," leading to journeyman status. I think these problems can be met if all who utilize the construction industry insist that these problems reflect, not only the interests of the unions, but also the interests of those whose buildings are beings built, and the public interest in equal employment opportunity.

Now I come to a crucial point. The contractors would like to increase the labor force, but they are under steady, unremitting pressure from the unions not to do so. They do not actively oppose civil rights actions, but will not antagonize the unions by supporting such actions. Thus, at the moment, the pressure for civil rights actions by the contractors comes only from the government. If you joined in that pressure, it would further your general interests.

But how can you do this? Action on a project by project basis by you is probably impracticable. I suggested that you do it by giving public and political support to these programs. Demand that the Department of Labor take action to increase minority participation in the building trades. If law suits are filed against our actions, join as amicus curiae to support our activities. When someone, such as the President of the sheetmetal workers, lashes out at a program which seeks to expand minority participation, use your great influence to support such programs. In this way, the public interest that you represent, and the interests in equal employment opportunity which I am obligated to protect, may succeed in reaching the objectives which we both seek.

APPENDIX C

National Goal—Equality and Parity in the Seventies

Address Before The Pennsylvania League of Cities, Philadelphia, Pennsylvania, August 11, 1969

It is a pleasure to address your 70th Annual Convention today. As a matter of fact, it is a pleasure just to be here with you, with people who are working at the local level to solve local problems.

I am a local government man myself. Before coming to work for The Federal Government, I was a City Councilman—in Pasco, Washington—and a Special Assistant for Urban Affairs to Governor Dan Evans of Washington State. When I leave The Department of Labor, I intend to return to the level of local, urban problems. Just to show you how deep my preferences for the local approach to problem-solving go, the man I chose as my deputy was previously a City Manager.

So I feel as if I am among friends who speak the same language. And I feel as if I see local urban problems about the same way as *you* do.

You have asked me to speak about "Civil Disorder" and the response of The Nixon Administration. Though I will touch on the recent flight to the moon, on the depression of the 1930s, and several other topics in the course of my remarks, I trust that

101

—in the end—you will see how what I will have said bears on the topic you assigned me.

I wonder if we all had the same thoughts as we watched the Apollo flight two weeks ago. I do not refer now to the superb technical achievement. That was simply awesome. The scientists developed new materials which were light and which could withstand the extraordinary heat. They developed a fantastically intricate set of machinery and instrumentation. Industry was able to build all of these to exacting specifications. And men—the hundreds of engineers, technicians, controllers and what have you, and the three courageous astronauts—were able to fly the ship to the moon and back, safely and successfully.

The technical achievement was incredible, and I am sure you marvelled at it as I did. But I confess that the most impressive aspect of Apollo, the most educational for me, was the *social* achievement. Did that strike you too?

The Apollo program involved the cooperation and commitment of literally millions of people over a long period of time. The first decision to enter manned space flight came in 1958, during Eisenhower's second term. In 1961, President Kennedy proposed that we land a man on the moon by the end of the decade. Last month we did so.

From the time the space program began until we landed Neil Armstrong and Edwin Aldrin on the moon, the national administration had changed three times. Five congressional elections had taken place. A President had been assasinated. The country passed through two recessions and then faced mounting inflation. We became involved in a major land war in Vietnam. We experienced unprecedented civil disorder.

But the space program continued. It continued even though eight of the first ten launches—including all of the first five— were failures. It continued even after the tragic launching pad deaths of three astronauts. And it was successful.

This nation succeeded in putting men on the moon because we set ourselves a clear, concrete, measurable goal. And it was a goal we reasonably could expect to achieve, by putting out our best efforts.

We set ourselves a concrete goal, and then we developed a timetable for achieving it. The timetable not only included a deadline for achievement of the goal, but also a number of intermediate checkpoint dates, by which time we expected to achieve various intermediate objectives.

To achieve our goal—and our intermediate objectives—within the established timetable, we carefully designed a detailed program. This program specified all the projects and activities we would have to work through. Most important, it enumerated the resources which would be required—not only the total financial cost, but also all the manpower and all the organizations and all the materials which would be needed. And if the program indicated, for instance, that we needed a new material with specified properties—a material not previously in existence—then the program also laid out when to start developing that new material, in order to have it ready when it was needed.

Apollo succeeded because we carefully and clearly specified goals, timetables, programs to achieve the goals within the timetables, and the resources required, including plans to develop resources needed but not yet in existence. We specified all the elements clearly, estimating as closely as we could, and then we agreed—*firmly*—that we were going to achieve the goal, period, and that we were going to *furnish* the *required resources, period*.

When NASA first asked Congress, in 1961, to approve the plans for a lunar landing, the estimated cost was $19 billion. The actual cost turned out to be about $24 Billion, some 25 percent greater than originally anticipated. We paid the additional $5 billion as a matter of course. We intended to put men on the moon by the end of the decade, and that is all there was to it.

The Apollo program is by no means the only national effort of this magnitude and this determination which we have undertaken. The Manhattan project—which developed awesomely effective atomic weaponry for the first time—was similar in complexity and in national commitment. So was the country's program to develop intercontinental ballistic missiles. So, in a sense, is our commitment to complete our inter-state highway system by 1975; this last, in fact, is even more expensive than the Apollo program. I have focused on the Apollo program here, because it has been much on our minds lately, and because I think it illustrates with special clarity the elements a major national effort must include, if it is to be succesful. As a man with a background in local government, and with a deep concern about urban problems, I would like to see this nation undertake the same kind of effort to respond to our needs in the cities.

The truth is that a great deal of talk would imply that some such program is already underway. The celebrated war on poverty is the best example of this kind of talk.

What you know, as the men on the local scene, and what I know too, is that our "Urban Program"—if I may use that phrase loosely—is in no way comparable to the Apollo Program. It is not comparable, for one thing, because the level of commitments has never conceived. It lacks those critical elements I spoke of earlier.

The failure to specify these elements clearly, as much as the inadequate level of investment, has led to the comparative ineffectuality of the war on poverty.

I think The Nixon Administration is doing a good deal to straighten out this problem of sloppiness in conception of goals and programs. In a few minutes I would like to talk with you about what I am doing along that line with The Office of Federal Contract Compliance, for which I am responsible. But first, let us explore some of our urban problems in some detail.

I am sure that most of you here remember the depression. Probably many of you were raised during that time, as I was. Probably some of you learned then what it was like to live in poverty, as I did, and probably some of you saw your parents doing all kinds of jobs for a living, which really did not make full use of their education and skills and experience.

Life was tough, then, and yet we all more or less accepted things the way they were. The depression was not pleasant, but I guess it seemed natural to us then.

When the war came, a lot of things changed. A lot of us went into the armed forces. At least, we were employed. What is more, a good many of us learned new job skills while in the service. And many of us returned and used our G.I. bill privileges to get technical training or a college education. The war opened up hundred of thousands of jobs at home too, especially in construction and in the factories.

I suppose the war led in some ways to a great improvement in life. That was particularly true for Negroes. Jobs got so plentiful at home that industry had to begin admitting us to trades which previously had been for whites only. Of course, Mr. Philip Randolph and some others did have to raise the possibility of a march on Washington before President Roosevelt ordered defense plants to hire blacks as well as whites. But in any case, many were opened to us. And thousands of us received an education we never would have got without the war.

So things looked pretty rosy for all Americans after the war, particularly after the fear of a new depression proved illfounded. Things looked especially rosy for black Americans. We figured we had fought for our country, we had proved our capabilities in the services and in the factories, and many of us subsequently had certified ourselves by earning college degrees.

As the sense of security and well-being grew, many Negroes invested in homes, once again proving that when the opportunities were available Negroes wanted to achieve just about the same kind of satisfaction in life as anyone else.

In the late forties and early fifties, however, black folks began to realize that their hopes were a little too optimistic. When those of us who developed our talents in college went looking for jobs which would use our capabilities, we found the doors closed. So, the post office greatly increased in its number of college-educated postmen.

The fellows who had found jobs in factories during the war or right after the war did somewhat better for awhile, They soon learned that Negroes could rise only so high generally not even to the level of foreman, thus shutting off their capacity to develop their skills and advance in accord with the "American Dream." But at least most of them were able to retain their jobs—until the mid-fifties, that is.

When the recession of those years began, it soon became clear that black people would be the first to be laid off. Most companies, in fact, had maintained separate seniority systems for blacks and whites, to avoid "threatening" their white workers. During the same period, the first round of automation began. Nineteen thousand black workers lost their jobs in the Chicago area when one company, Armour, automated. Hundreds of homes were foreclosed, after years of scrimping and hoping. And this sad process was repeated by the employees of numerous other companies.

With these experiences, the hopes of Negroes were destroyed. The despair, hopelessness, and frustration which had entered the black community when the colleage-educated Negroes could not find jobs, spread much more widely.

I do not want to exaggerate what happened. Many black factory workers retained their jobs, and some Negroes educated under the G. I. Bill had been able to find adequate employment. The economic state of the black community, as a whole never fell to as low a point as it had during the depression, though the Negro unemployment rate was consistently twice as high as the white rate, and the median Negro earnings figure was only 55% of the white figure.

For many Negroes, the fifties were a time of disillusionment. The hopes we had built during the forties were destroyed. Many of us—those who had never shared in the progress of the forties, and those who lost what they had gained—were living in poverty. Many, many more were employed in jobs which called on only a small part of their capabilities.

Much of the black community had slipped back into an economic state of depression. This time, however, we could see that it was not a natural event, because the rest of the country was living in prosperity. Only conscious discrimination could explain the depression-level state of many in the black population.

In these years we went home in the evenings and we cursed and we fumed and we damned "whitey" from one end of the house to the other. These were just the years when we were raising our children, born in the "baby boom" of the forties.

In some instances we were aware, but in most instances we were not aware that we were raising the young black militants who are on the streets today. These are our offspring, and much of their bitterness, and much of their indifference to education stems from the fact that they knew their fathers—and often their mothers too—were qualified to hold good jobs and were being denied those jobs. As a classroom teacher—which I was, during those years—I can tell you how hard it was to try to convince some of those youngsters that they should go ahead and develop their human resources in spite of the fact that there might not be a job opportunity out there.

Now if you had canvassed the black community in the late

forties, you wouldn't have found anyone who would suggest that integration was't worth pursuing. Our hopes were still bound up with the idea that once a black man has developed himself to the point where he can be a productive citizen, this society and this system is so designed that he'll get to use that skill.

When the present generation was canvassed in Detroit, only a few months ago, some 28 percent of the young blacks were committed to separatism. That is quite a change. Of course most of the rest were still committed to integration: they still believed we could make it. The answer to the question of integration or separatism is still hanging in the balance.

The real test, so far as I am concerned, is the next generation: the one that is being raised now, in the sixties. "Things are getting better," we so often hear these days, and it probably is true. But these kids have also seen the assassinations of Martin Luther King, Medgar Evers, Malcolm X, John and Robert Kennedy and scores of less well-known people like Emmitt Till. They have seen little more than token integration in most of their schools, fifteen years after the Brown Vs. Board of Education decision. They may have noticed that 80 percent of the whites polled in that Detroit survey said they wanted nothing more than token integration.

What do you think the labor market looks like to these kids, as they start looking for jobs? The unemployment rate for teenage black males is well over 20 percent: no wonder some drop out of school, some turn to hustling, and some turn to the panthers. The rate for teen-age black females is as high as in the 1930's. It does not seem that the much-discussed stabilizing influence of the Negro female is likely to hold up much longer, if that kind of employment experience continues.

If we lose this generation to frustration and despair, I am afraid we may lose the ball game. We may lose, first of all, because the rapidly advancing technological revolution which has already locked many adult Negroes in permanent poverty will leave these unprepared youngsters too far behind to recover. We may lose, second, because this new generation—on top of the present generation of black militants—simply will not listen any longer to our insistence that things are getting better, no matter how many times we repeat it.

Again, I do not want to exaggerate the picture. A good many Negroes—perhaps as many as a third or even a half—are making moderately good incomes and finding slightly less rigid barriers to advancement than those which existed ten and twenty years ago.

But the rest of the black population is living in a depressed state which might well be compared to an under-developed economy. People's capabilities are not being fully used. Capital with which to build the economy is scarce. The terms of trade with the wider economy are overbalanced against the black community. Of course the analogy of the under-developed economy is particularly apt today, as the poverty ridden-portion of the Negro community solidifies in isolated ghettoes.

This is the point at which The Office of Federal Contract Compliance comes in. The Federal Government pays private industry literally billions of dollars to purchase all kinds of goods and services. Last year it paid out something like $20 billion dollars to the construction industry alone.

The Government has control over all those dollars at only one point—the point at which they pass from the government's hands into the hands of the contractors. Once those dollars flow on from the contractor into the community, the Government has nothing to say about how they are used.

Historically, as we all know, those dollars from federal contracts flowed from the contractors into the hands of white workers and white suppliers. They in turn spent the money in white supermarkets, clothing stores, banks, etc. When those white merchants spent their incomes, they too shopped in white business.

With minor exceptions, the under-developed black community I mentioned a moment ago was left out of this economic cycle which began with the federal contract. White-owned companies got the contracts, they hired white workers and subcontracted with white companies, and from there on out blacks didn't have a chance.

That's a prime example of institutionalized racism. No one really specified that those federal dollars should circulate only in the white community, or support only the white economy, leaving the black community impoverished and economically isolated. But that's what happened.

The OFCC stands at the gate, where those federal dollars flow to the contractor, and into the economy as a whole. It stands at the one point where the government can affect the use of those dollars, where it can either close its eyes and let those dollars continue to support institutional racism, or where—if it chooses —it can see that all groups in our society—Mexican-Americans, Puerto Ricans, Blacks, Chinese- and Japanese-Americans, as well as whites—have full opportunity to share in their benefits. The Government can see that federal dollars have a fair chance of supporting the black, Mexican-American, and Puerto Rican economies, as well as the white one.

In the end, of course, what we all want is one big economy, in which all of us participate fully. All I'm saying is that to get there, we have to see to it that a fair share of the federal dollars spent on procurement flows through the hands of people of all groups in our society. Then everyone will have the resources to choose whatever place he wants in the national economy.

In the past the OFCC has asked the contractors voluntarily to see that part of that money flowed into minority economies, as well as the white economy. In some trades and some industries, very significant advances have occurred by virture of private, voluntary initiative. In others, little progress has been made.

This is where the lessons of the Apollo program come to bear. We got to the moon because we committed ourselves to clearly-established goals. I believe those same lessons can fruitfully be applied to our domestic problems, and specifically to this problem of minority group employment.

Our first test of this "Apollo" approach is being made right here in Philadelphia. Just over a month ago I announced a Philadelphia Plan for the construction industry in this area, which establishes—for the first time—specific goals and timetables for minority group employment. It applies to seven designated trades in which clear patterns of discrimination exist. All construction contractors in this five-county area working on federally-assisted projects will be expected to make every effort to hire members of minority groups in the seven trades, within ranges we will specify soon.

The Federal Government plans to invest approximately $600 million dollars in some 38 construction projects in this area in the next two years. This activity will provide jobs for an estimated

22,500 men. If the contractors comply fully with our established ranges, some 325 to 500 men of minority groups will receive jobs, who probably would not have received them otherwise, and perhaps $2 million in wages will flow into the economy of the minority community. Given the multiplier effect, that might generate $10 million in additional income in the minority community. In addition, we hope those men—through their new experience in major commercial construction—will find a permanent place in the industry.

All these numbers are quite modest, as I am sure you will agree. That is because we are focusing only on seven construction trades where discrimination is particularly severe. Most of these trades have admitted less than 1-1/2 percent blacks, in a city whose racial make-up is about 20 percent black. Furthermore, our goals in these seven trades are modest, in order to assure that contractors will be able to meet them.

To be certain that we leave no possibility for voluntary action unexamined, we have delayed announcing the specific ranges and timetables while we explore with union and contractor representatives—both here and in Washington—the possibility of their undertaking a concerted affirmative action program—with goals and timetables established by them, in lieu of our plan. We are most hopeful that their interest will bear fruit. If not, we are prepared to go ahead with the Philadelphia Plan as it stands.

Parenthetically I should comment that the comptroller-general has offered an opinion that this Philadelphia Plan is inconsistent with some provisions of The Civil Rights Act.

Naturally we don't share this view. Neither does The U. S. Attorney General. We do think it important, however, that the plan be given a trial here in order to test its workability. We believe it will work and we hope those who now may be critical of the plan will change their views as the plan demonstrates its ability to achieve its objectives.

We hope to develop similar plans elsewhere, as soon as we have been able to observe how well this plan is working here.

In the past few minutes, I have tried to describe for you how the Office of Federal Contract Compliance works, and what approach it is pursuing at present. So far I've spoken only of the initiatives we are taking in Washington.

As we advance the work of the OFCC across the country, we intend to offer increasing responsibility in evolving goals, time-tables, and programs to local leaders. We plan to offer the resources of The Department of Labor in support, and to monitor the progress of local programs. But we hope the cities will want to take increasing responsibility in this area themselves.

The Federal Government simply cannot involve itself in man-power planning in every city in the country. It cannot even develop the framework, a Philadelphia Plan, for every city in the country. It doesn't have the resources, and basically it's not the right level of government anyway.

Every city in the country should be involved in manpower planning. The cities are making the efforts to attract new industry. The cities are where the neighborhoods of poverty are located. Only the cities really have the kind of information that is required to do a consistently effective job of manpower planning.

Let us take Harrisburg as an example. The Commonwealth of Pennsylvania's Bureau of Employment security has projected the creation of approximately 11,000 new jobs in the Harrisburg area between 1970 and 1975. (The City Government may have even more reliable data, but this state-sponsored study is a good starting point.) Those 11,000 new jobs are broken down into approximately 400 in the construction trades, 100 operatives, 3000 in clerical occupations, and so on—into some 147 different occupational categories, in fact.

When you have determined the approximate numbers and kinds of jobs which will be opening, you turn to the supply side, to find out who is going to be available to fiill those jobs. Are there apprentice and other training programs to develop 40 new construction tradesmen within 5 years? How about operatives? If not enough operatives are going to be available, what can be done to produce them? You want to fit training output as closely as possible to the job opportunities expected to be available.

After these steps are taken care of, you go back and ask how many residents, white and non-white, need jobs. How many graduates of high school and of all training programs will there be? Do all of these people have a full opportunity to enter one of the occupational categories with a projected deficit? Do people of

111

all races have an equal chance to enter the more attractive occupations?

In order to deal effectively with those poverty neighborhoods it is critically important that you assure their residents ample opportunity to take advantage of the new jobs opening up. All too often in the past those residents have been by-passed and excluded, and their poverty and their frustration have deepened. Only men at the local level, like yourselves, really know what these problems are in *your* communities, and how they can be attacked.

Now once you have diagnosed your real situation, you are ready to prepare your own "Apollo Program" concerning manpower. Your goals should include full utilization of minority manpower. Then come timetables in which to meet them and a specification of the resources required.

Then you will have two selling jobs to do. The easiest will be selling the unemployed and the youth on preparing themselves for the expanding occupations. The harder one, perhaps, will be selling your approach to local employers, and to new industrialists whom you expect to come in and invest in your town.

The approach to these employers, as I am sure you have found, must be directed. They must understand the point of your program, and then they must clearly commit themselves to full cooperation with it.

This is the point where the idea of local initiative in manpower planning may become a little unsettling for you. It seems to me, though, that times are changing now. Most of the large firms are beginning to realize their responsibility to help solve our serious social problems by opening jobs to those who previously were excluded. Today, some firms will probably look on a city's carefully-developed manpower program as a sign of constructive concern.

Beyond these posibilities, you should remember that the expectations established by the OFCC apply to all federal contractors everywhere. So the company which decides to invest in Tennessee, let us say, rather than Pennsylvania, will have to live up to pretty much the same requirements. Only he will not have, perhaps, the benefit of local assistance in living up to them.

Another concern you may have—in evaluating the idea of undertaking manpower planning programs locally—is the problem of resources. Resources can be a problem, but only for some aspects of your program. Seeing that employers hire all qualified applicants on an equal opportunity basis is not very costly at all, and I assure you that its payoff is great, both to the man who gets the job and to the community in which he spends his income. Furthermore, the Labor Department's Manpower administration is most anxious to fit its programs to local plans and local needs. I am sure its cooperation will be a tremendous resource.

For the last fifteen years—for the past 100 years, in fact—people have been saying: "Things are getting better. The condition of the Negro in America is improving. Progress is on its way." This theme is a favorite of white politicians at election time, but I've heard it from all sides—from white businessmen, from "concerned liberals," from college professors, even from black civil rights leaders on occasion. "Things are getting better," everybody keeps saying. I agree. I'm sure almost everyone agrees. Things indeed are getting better.

The problem is that, "getting better" no longer is *good enough.* After fifteen years—after an entire *century,* if we really want to face the truth squarely—people are beginning to ask: "Yeah, but how much better? What have we really accomplished?" And some are going one step further, and they are asking: "When does the process of getting better actually arrive at the goal of what is good, what is just, and what is right?" These are fair questions.

Fours years from now, I want to be able to look back and actually see what we have accomplished, for my own satisfaction and for the satisfaction of all those people asking these questions. Even more, I want to be sure we *have* accomplished something.

In the light of the variety of urban problems this country must face, the office of federal contract compliance may seem to have a fairly small role. In a sense it does. But I think its role is not so much limited by its charter to focus on equal employment by government contractors, as it is limited by the necessity to rely on *local action* to actually *assure* equal employment opportunity throughout the country. But the necessity to rely on local action is a limitation I like.

I have already explained to you how central equal employment is to the whole process of offering true progress to the underdeveloped minority economies of the country, and to the people who live in them. Equal employment offers jobs to the unemployed. It creates opportunities for further realization of potential on the part of the underemployed. In short, it squarely attacks the economic and human problems of underutilized resources. At the same time, through salaries and wages for work performed, equal employment can provide major amounts of additional capital for use in the underdeveloped economies of the minority communities. And when we realize that federal contractors account for fully a third of the total jobs in this country, we see that the OFCC has plenty of leverage on the problem.

If you establish goals and timetables and if you commit the necessary resources and all your own energies, if you resolve that neither inflation nor recession, political change nor civil disorder will deter you from achieving the goals within the established timetables, then you will be on the road to solving our urban problems. And if you don't assume this responsibility, in your own communities, nothing else you do, and nothing The Federal Government does— neither all the resources it might expend nor all the regulations it might establish—will save you, or us.

APPENDIX D
Contemporary Racism

Address Before The United Presbyterian Church General Assembly, Rochester, New York, May 24, 1971

I appreciate the honor which you have bestowed upon me by asking me to address you on the most important moral questions of our time. Questions which go directly to the future of our form of government, and the question of whether the fundamental moral values which underly the Judeo-Christian traditions of America will be realized by our children.

I have reviewed, in great detail, the document which you are considering, entitled: "The Report of the Council on Church and Race to the 183rd General Assembly," with the sub-title "Racism and Repression." I want to speak to several aspects of that report. I will do so from two perspectives: First, as Assistant Secretary of Labor, I am responsible for the enforcement of executive order 11246, which prohibits racial, ethnic and sex discrimination by government contractors and requires affirmative action to provide equal employment opportunity. In that capacity, I daily have the opportunity to observe, and sometimes pass upon, a whole range of industrial relations practices, which have the effect of restricting minority employment opportunity. Thus, my understanding of the pattern of discrimination in the land is sharpened by the work I do every day, by the materials and discussions in which I am involved. In addition, I can observe how the government responds to these problems of employment discrimination and to other problems of discrimination, because I sometimes participate in governmental activities in this area which goes beyond supervision of the Office of Federal Contract Compliance, which enforces the executive order with respect to government contractors.

The second perspective from which I can speak, is as a black American, who has experienced the range of restrictive practices in my own life, seen my future, and my family's future shaped— no, warped—by the pattern of discrimination which is the subject of the report. As one of a very limited number of blacks who have "made it" in this administration, I have a perspective of the whole of America on the race question.

The first comment I wish to make is that the first paragraph of the report accurately describes racism and its consequences.

"Racism assumes the inferiority of nonwhites as a group and relegates them, on the basis on skin color, language or cultural differences, to the lowest status in the social, economic, political and religious life of the nation. Racism has been the chief cause of the disproportionate poverty of Blacks, Spanish-Speaking minorities and American Indians ... And is, therefore, the basic factor in the social and psychological damage these groups have experienced historically in American society. It is today the single most important source of traditional and non-traditional devices which are used everyday in the overt and covert oppression of the black, brown, red and to a lesser degree, yellow minorities in the United States."

This paragraph is correct. And, it is the key to understanding the rest of the document. The Kerner Report, on the riots of 1967, pointed out the growth of racism as a danger to America. The task force on race and minority group relations for the White House Conference of youth, confirmed and strengthened the conclusion that racism is a major responsible agent for the position of minority Americans.

Moving to the area in which I have jurisdiction and experience, I want to cite to you a document of fundamental importance, which has been largely ignored by the press, and often ignored by policy makers. The fact that this document is ignored so frequently, while its relevance to the approach to employment discrimination is so obvious, is itself a manifestation of the subtle "Look the other way" form of racism which we find so often in the more sophisticated sectors of our society.

This document is called "The Many Faces of Job Discrimination." It appears at the beginning of the three volumes of statistics on racial discrimination in employment for 1966, published by the equal employment opportunity commission under the title "Job Patterns for Minorities and Women in Private Industry."

It has recently been reproduced as chapter 3 of Rutgers Law Professor Alfred W. B. Blumrosen's book, *Black Employment and the Law*. In essence, this statistical analysis discloses that, at the most, *one third* of the discrimination and subordinate positions in employment held by minorities can be attributed to deficiencies in education and training compared to the white majority. The remaining *two-thirds* is attributed to discrimination. Now, the policy implications of this report, for government action, are extraordinary and powerful. If two-thirds of the problem resides in connection with discrimination, then we must wipe out that discrimination with vigorous law enforcement. The budget, staff, research and technical apparatus to enforce the law must be enlarged and sharpened. If one-third of the discrimination is due to education and training deficiences, then we should allocate no more than one-third of our total available resources to this field. Since it costs far more to develop and implement training programs than it does to develop and implement law enforcement programs, it seems clear that the bulk of our resources should go for the moment to law enforcement, because that will produce the greatest payoff.

But this conclusion is ignored, while the white community continues to seek to believe that the depressed condition of minorities is either their own fault, or is due to defiiciencies in education and training. The failure to recognize that the deficiencies are due to discrimination itself, then contributes to policies which limit the resources for the battle against discrimination.

It is this vicious circle, in which the pattern of discrimination is so profound that it prohibits people from recognizing the discrimination that causes nearly total frustration, often erroneous policy decisions and the resultant failure to implement our great moral and legal principles concerning the equality of men and the individuality of each of us.

Put concretely, most of the good men among us will say that they do not discriminate. What they mean is that they do not have personal dislike for Blacks or Spanish-speaking persons, and would not maliciously do them harm. Yet, daily, they participate in the administration of systems in employment, housing, finance, social activities and, sometimes even religious activities, which have the effect of excluding minorities and perpetuating their subordinate position. They locate factories in all-white suburban communities, and post notices of job vacancies at the gate. They utilize tests which screen out most minorities from opportunities, without demonstrating that the tests measure abiliy to do the job, rather than the ability to pass the test. They build all-white suburban housing developments, and give loans only in areas which will be occupied by whites. None of these things is done with malice. They are all done for "other reasons." But the consequences are the same. And such men will say, in all apparent honesty—for their own racism forbids them to recognize the contrary—that they are not discriminating at all. They have defined discrimination narrowly, so that their own activities are beyond that concept. And I will state, that if their narrow definition of discrimination is accepted generally, then none of our laws will address, much less solve, the social problems of our times; and the holocaust forecast in the report, which we are looking at today, is nearly upon us.

Yet, I also have to report to you that after some thirty years of state and Federal Fair Employment Practice Laws being on the books but not enforced, we finally have a legal definition of discrimination, which deals with the issue of intent; and resolves the question of whether morally innocent acts which have the effect of suppressing minorities constitute discrimination. The supreme court of the United States, speaking through Chief Justice Warren Burger, in *Griggs V. Duke Power Company* (91 S. Ct. 849) addressed this issue in the folowing terms:

"The objective of Congress in the enactment of Title VII (The Employment Discrimination Provision of the Civil Rights Act of 1964) . . . was to achieve equality of employment opportunities and remove barriers that have operated in the past to favor an identifiable group of white employees over other employees. Under the act, practices, procedures or tests neutral on their face, and even neutral in terms of intent, cannot be maintained if they operate to "freeze" the status quo of prior discriminatory employment practices.

". . . The act proscribes not only overt discrimination but also practices that are fair in form, but discriminatory in operation. The touchstone is business necessity. If an employment practice which operates to exclude Negroes cannot be shown to be related to jobs performance, the practice is prohibited.

". . . Good intent or the absence of discriminatory intent does not redeem employment procedures or testing mechanisms that operate as "built in headwinds" for minority groups and are unrelated to measuring job capability.

". . . Congress directed the thrust of the act to the *consequences* of employment practices, not simply the motivation."

The court faced, and squarely rejected, the notion that discrimination required an evil motive, a desire or purpose to harm minorities.

The thrust of this definition is applicable under most Federal and State statutes and under The President's executive order against discrimination by government contractors. It condemns as discriminatory a whole range of recruiting, hiring and promotion practices in employment, and equally the tenant selection practices of landlords who operate segregated apartments and continue their segregated character by filling vacancies in a manner which has the effect of excluding minorities. It also condemns developers of private housing, whose marketing practices have the effect of creating all white suburban areas, and employers locating new plants in areas which are likely to produce an all-white labor force. It finally condemns builders and contractors, who do business with unions which they know will send them all white workers. All of these practices, and many more, stand condemned under the definition of discrimination laid down by Chief Justice Burger. In the field of implementing Civil Rights legislation in housing and employment, the decision in *Griggs V. Duke Power Co.* is the most important single act ever performed by the Supreme Court of the United States.

I submit to you that the statements of Chief Justice Burger are parallel to the thrust of the first paragraph of the racism and repression report, and reflect an acute understanding of the systematic nature of discrimination in our society. Perhaps this is an occasion when the law has moved into a position to influence the morality of the community.

The next specific point I would like to make is with reference to a paragraph of the report which suggests that the problem of racism cannot be addressed by "token representation" and "minor adjustments in the society."

As far as tokenism is concerned, its day is indeed done. When I came into office, it was still true that large corporations in America could satisfy their federal obligations toward equality of employment oportunity, by hiring token niggers and having them sit by the door when the government man came by. And the "House Nigger" on the Board of Advisors of The White Institution was a common phenomenon. "Liberal" institutions would have a few Negroes around to demonstrate their liberalism. These days are going. The Philadelphia Plan for equal employment opportunity in the construction trades involves the imposition of specific numerical goals and timetables for minority participation in those trades which have discriminated for so long. This plan has now been upheld by the court of appeals for The Third Circuit.

The plan destroys tokenism, by making specific numerical requirements on the contractor as the price of his doing federal business. I hope that these numerical requirements can soon be done away with, because I, along with all of you, want to come into the era where individuals are treated on their individual merits. Yet, our experience is conclusive—that if we do not use goals and targets, the pattern of racism will persist, and minorities will continue to be excluded. Thus, the pattern of racism itself forces us to take these steps.

Program implementation along these lines does take some time, and the result is that the tradition of tokenism is still understood by the minority community to be in fact the response of industry, government and other circles. Only a vast network of visible government actions can overcome the impression that tokenism is national policy: an impression based on generations of experience.